Mythology
OF THE WORLD

NEIL PHILIP
MYTHOLOGY
OF THE WORLD

KINGFISHER

FOR SINÉAD PHILIP

KINGFISHER

Kingfisher Publications Plc, New Penderel House
283–288 High Holborn, London WC1V 7HZ
www.kingfisherpub.com

First published by Kingfisher Publications Plc in 2004
10 9 8 7 6 5 4 3 2 1

1TR/0604/PROSP/CLSN(CLSN)/157MA/F

Publishing manager: Melissa Fairley
Senior designer: Jane Tassie
Picture research manager: Cee Weston-Baker
DTP manager: Nicky Studdart
Senior production controller: Lindsey Scott
Artwork archivists: Wendy Allison, Jenny Lord
Proofreader: Sheila Clewley
Indexer: Sue Lightfoot

A CIP catalogue record for this book is available
from the British Library.

ISBN 0 7534 0964 X

Printed in China

MAP KEY

Grasslands   Broadleaf forests   Rainforests

Deserts   Mountains   Tundra

Needleleaf forests   Polar lands

CONTENTS

Introduction

A myth is first and foremost a story. But it is a story
that encodes the values, beliefs and dreams of a people,
so each myth arises from a particular cultural context.
The sacred qualities of the myths are central to the meaning of
each story. Often myths may only be told by certain individuals,
or at certain times of the year, or during certain rituals or
ceremonies. To re-tell or re-enact a myth is to step out of
this world and into the myth world.

The myth world is one in which the powerful
unseen forces that shape and animate the everyday
world live. A myth is a way of understanding
or negotiating with those forces to create
a pathway between the two worlds.

This book offers a glimpse into a few of these myth worlds, and into the worlds of the myth-makers. Some cultures may be poor by material standards, but their myths are rich in imaginative beauty.

In one myth of the Akimel O'odham of the American southwest (see pages 112–113), the god Buzzard creates a whole miniature world, with a sun, moon and stars, just like our world. Each myth is like this miniature cosmos of Buzzard's. Within it is a whole world, complete in every detail. A single myth could take a lifetime to explore, yet still remain a mystery.

Myths are many-layered and rich in meaning. They are a vehicle for the deepest truths that human beings are able to understand or express. So although myths are best understood in the context of the society that created them, they are also a treasure that belongs to all humanity. We forget or ignore them at our peril.

Neil Philip

NORTH
AMERICA

ATLANTIC
OCEAN

PACIFIC OCEAN

SOUTH
AMERICA

THE
WORLD

N
W E
S

What are myths?

Myths are sacred stories. The word myth comes from the ancient Greek word muthos, meaning 'a story'. The myths of the ancient Greeks are among the best-known such stories. They tell of the doings of the supreme god Zeus and the other gods of Mount Olympus (see pages 34–35), and of the deeds of great heroes such as Herakles and Theseus (see pages 36–37).

The Nuxalk Nation of British Columbia (ritual mask, above) thought of their world as a flat circular island, which was kept stable by a supernatural being, Sninia, who held it steady with a rope. When Sninia adjusted his grip, earthquakes occurred. In the flat land above their world lived the gods, in the House of Myths.

Vishnu, the preserver, is one of the most important of the Hindu gods. Nine times he has come to earth in human or animal form to help humankind. His first such form was Matsya, the fish, the appearance he took to protect Manu (see page 75), the first man, from the flood.

THE MATSYA AVATAR.

Similar stories

One Greek myth tells of Zeus (see pages 30–31) opening the heavens to let rain flood the earth. Two beings, Deukalion and Pyrrha, escape in an ark and create a new race when the ark comes to rest on the summit of Mount Parnassus. This flood myth is similar to the Biblical story of Noah and the flood. That story in turn is remarkably like the earlier Mesopotamian flood myth, in which the survivor of the flood was called Ziusidra by the Sumerians (see page 68), and Utnapishtim by the Babylonians.

Across the world in India, a Hindu myth tells how the god Brahma took the form of a fish (see page 75) in order to protect Manu, the first man. The myth of a great flood can be found almost all over the world except for Africa. Even the Aboriginal peoples of Australia, who had no cultural contact with the rest of humanity for tens of thousands of years, have flood myths. The destruction of the world by flood or fire, along with its re-populating with a new race of humanity, is just one of the great universal themes of myth. Myths tell how the world was created, how humanity came into being, and how we learned to live in the world and make use of its natural resources.

The myth of the twins Romulus and Remus (see pages 44–45), who were brought up by a wolf (left) and then a shepherd, was the symbolic foundation stone of the Roman empire. The annual festival of purification, known as Lupercalia, was a ritual race around the furrows first ploughed by Romulus. It started with a sacrifice of goats at the Lupercal cave, where the wolf nurtured the twins.

Various ways to tell myths

In cultures which believe in many gods and spirits, mythologies can become very complex. And because myths act as a kind of foundation for social and cultural beliefs and practices, different sections of a society may tell different myths. An example of this is the case of the Ngarrindjeri Aboriginal people (see pages 136–137), where mythology exists both as a shared body of belief and as secret knowledge known only to either the men or the women.

Myths can be told as stories, or expressed in art, song, ritual or dance. Many cultures hold ceremonies in which dancers impersonate the gods. In the Nuxalk Nation of British Columbia (see pages 106–107), for instance, two secret societies, the Sisaok and the Kusiut, were responsible for dramatized dances known as the Winter Ceremonial Season. The dancers wore elaborate wooden masks, representing the gods who live above this world in the House of Myths.

Among the Marind-Anim of southern Papua New Guinea, ritual dancers (left) represent the déma, ancestral spirits who lived in the mythical creation-time. Like the ancestral beings of the Aboriginal Dreaming (see pages 134–135), the déma are half-man, half-animal. To the Marind-Anim, the invisible world of the déma is more important and more real than the visible world in which they live.

MYTH AND CULTURE

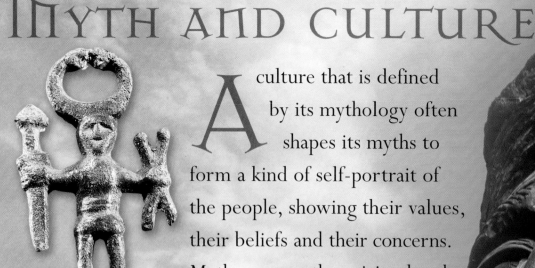

A culture that is defined by its mythology often shapes its myths to form a kind of self-portrait of the people, showing their values, their beliefs and their concerns. Myths express the spiritual and intellectual life of people, and the content of the myths is a key to understanding how these people think.

The Vikings believed that Odin (above, see pages 58–59) and his brothers created the first people from driftwood logs of ash and elm. But it is another god, Heimdall, who is regarded as the culture hero.

SUPERHUMAN BEINGS

Most mythologies feature culture heroes – gods or superhuman beings who may steal the sun for humankind, bring the gift of fire, teach the people how to hunt, how to grow food, and how to weave baskets and cloth. Often these culture heroes institute religious ceremonies in which the myths that record this sacred knowledge are re-enacted.

Sometimes the culture hero is the same as the creator god, but often he or she is a less remote and unapproachable being, sometimes half-deity and half-human. For instance, in ancient Mesopotamia, the king of Uruk, Gilgamesh (see pages 72–73), was not just a culture hero, but the founding father of a whole society. Gilgamesh was one-third a man and two-thirds a god.

One important trickster culture hero is Maui (right), who, according to mythology, fished up the Pacific islands of Polynesia from the bottom of the ocean, pushed up the heavens, stole fire from the underworld, and snared the sun to slow it down and give humankind more daylight.

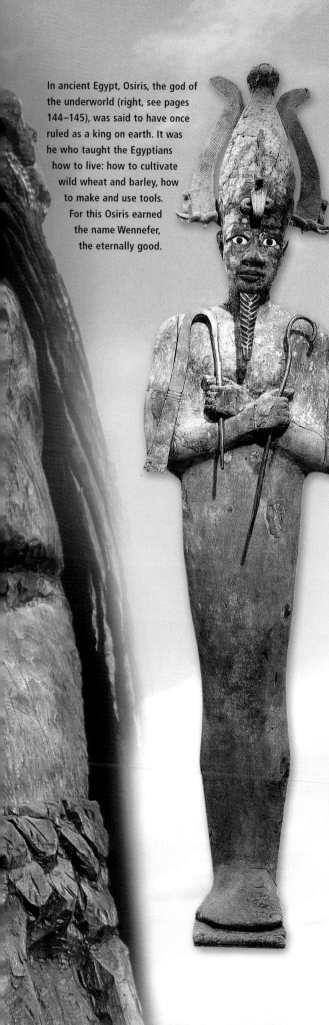

In ancient Egypt, Osiris, the god of the underworld (right, see pages 144–145), was said to have once ruled as a king on earth. It was he who taught the Egyptians how to live: how to cultivate wild wheat and barley, how to make and use tools. For this Osiris earned the name Wennefer, the eternally good.

TRICKSTER CULTURE HEROES

In many myths, the discovery of knowledge is related to the human characteristics of curiosity and playfulness, and this is reflected in the nature of many culture heroes, who are often described as tricksters. The native American tricksters take various animal or bird forms, such as a coyote or a raven. Spider Woman is an important goddess of the native American peoples of the southwest, such as the Navajo. She is a helper and teacher of humankind, but also dangerous and unpredictable, with the power to give and take life. In the myths of the Keres, she is known as Thinking Woman, the creator who spun this world from her thoughts.

The Nuxalk Nation (see pages 106–107) believed that the first ancestors of humanity descended to earth in animal form. With them was the trickster Raven, who was to be their teacher. But his actions were not always beneficial.

THE GIFT OF STORY

The trickster culture hero of the Asante of Ghana, Africa, is Ananse, the spider-man, who won the folktales from the sky god Onyankopon. This gift of stories shows that a culture hero does not simply arrange the world or teach crafts and skills, he or she is also the source of art and entertainment.

One Canadian Inuit myth tells how a young man, Teriak, brought back from the eagle-people the greatest gift of all: the gift of joy. The eagles taught Teriak how to hold a song festival, and now it is the duty of human beings to sing and be merry, for their joyful sounds will rise up from the earth to make old eagles young again.

Myth and spirituality

Because myths are sacred stories, often told or re-enacted in religious rituals, it is almost impossible to make a strict division between mythology and religion. Mythical gods and spirits are worshipped and feared as real beings. To a society that identifies itself completely with its mythology – such as a traditional tribal culture like that of the Ifugao of the Philippines – every action in this world has an echo in that of the gods.

The myths of the Australian Aboriginal peoples tell of the Rainbow Snake which created the hills, valleys and waterways of the ancestral landscape. This great snake now arches above the land as a rainbow, and can be seen reflected in water and in quartz. Aboriginal shamans or 'men of high degree' (left) obtain their powers from the Rainbow Snake, and manipulate them through the use of quartz crystals, for instance, to make rain.

Many gods

The Ifugao live in the mountainous central Cordillera, on Luzon island. Their huge rice terraces around Banaue have been called the eighth wonder of the world. The Ifugao believe that Field-Makers, hero ancestors, taught them to build their terraces.

Today, there are around 120,000 Ifugaos. The majority still honour their 1,500 separate gods. Such an impressive number of highly specialized gods is not unknown in other cultures. The ancient Romans had a god for almost everything, including a goddess of door hinges. The ancient Egyptians believed that there were so many gods they could not be numbered.

The human longing for eternal life is reflected in the Chinese Taoist myths of the Eight Immortals (left). These were great sages whose wisdom and virtue earned them eternal life with the gods, feasting on the peaches of immortality. Only one of them, He Xiangu, is a woman.

Shamans

Complex societies such as those of the ancient Egyptians, the Aztecs or the Incas had a whole class of priests to mediate between the human world and the world of the gods. In tribal societies, this task often falls to individuals known as shamans, who have acquired magical powers from the gods or spirits. The main responsibility of shamans is to heal the sick, which is why they have also been called medicine men or witch doctors.

The sibyls of ancient Greece (above) were prophetesses inspired by the god Apollo (see pages 40–41). The sibyl of Cumae in Campania accompanied Aeneas to the underworld, in search of his father Anchises. But when Aeneas found his father and tried to hug him, his arms closed on empty air.

Many native American shamans (Secotan shaman drawn in 1585, right) get their powers in vision quests, in which they gain the aid of a spirit helper. The bird fixed to this shaman's hair probably represents his spirit helper, giving him the ability to 'fly' while in a trance state.

Ancient skills

Shamanism is a very ancient model of human religious thought, dating back to the Stone Age (see page 29). Shamanic rituals are thought to lie behind the remarkable cave paintings and rock art of the European Ice Age (see page 28). Even into relatively modern times European peoples have practised various kinds of shamanism, for instance the ancient Greek seeresses known as sibyls, or the Viking warriors (see pages 58–59) who entered a 'berserk' battle frenzy when possessed by Odin.

The word shaman comes from Siberia, where shamanism was first fully studied, but shamanism is a worldwide spiritual tool. In southern Africa, the San people of the Kalahari desert believed that the trickster god /Kaggen (see pages 146–147) created the world by dreaming it into being. San shamans enter this same creative dream-state to exercise their mystical powers, such as rain-making and healing.

MYTH AND SOCIETY

Myths are sacred stories, but they are also tied in with the social structure of a society, its ideas about family, the development of its arts and crafts, all of which can be seen through its mythology. Myths provide a pathway into the world of the sacred, and a guide to how to live in this world.

The myth of the Hittite fertility god Telepinus (Hittite god, left) tells how he disappeared in a rage, so angry he put his shoes on the wrong feet, making the world barren. Only the annual rituals of humankind ensured that each year Telepinus would return to make the world fruitful again.

For the Tikigaq people of Point Hope, Alaska, myth was the living link between the people, the land, and the whales on which they depended for their survival. The Tikigaq peninsula was believed to have been a whale, which was harpooned by the god Raven in the creation-time and became the land. This myth had profound resonance for Tikigaq society and culture. While the Tikigaq men hunted the whale, they re-enacted the part of Raven. Meanwhile, the women remained in the igloo, re-enacting the part of the whale's soul. When the whale was landed, the wife of the successful hunter went down to the shore to welcome the dead whale to her family. An annual cycle of ritual and myth led up each year to the great spring whale hunt.

LIVING MYTHS

Myths are often viewed as a combination of religion and imagination, while their cultural and practical implications are ignored. This underestimates the extent to which myth permeates right through a society.

The Dogon of Mali in West Africa have one of the most complex mythological systems. Every village is regarded as a living person, lying north to south with the smithy at its head and shrines at its feet, because the creator Amma made the world from clay in the form of a woman lying in this position. The hut of the Hogon, the headman, is a model of the universe, and his movements within it are attuned to the rhythms of the universe; his pouch is 'the pouch of the world', and his staff is 'the axis of the world'. Every detail of his clothing relates to the creator god Amma, his twin sons the Nommo, or the world egg from which the cosmos was born.

The spiritual life of a Dogon village is rich and intense precisely because of the way in which the world of myth and the world the Dogon live in are intertwined.

MYTH AND FERTILITY

The necessity of ensuring the fertility of crops lies at the heart of much mythology, and there are numerous myths in which men or gods must plead with an angry god or goddess to relent and bring light, rain or fertility back to the land. The Japanese sun goddess Amaterasu (see pages 90–91) must be lured from her cave to bring back the sun; the Hittite fertility god Telepinus must be coaxed back from the mountain top or the drought will continue; the Greek goddess Demeter (see pages 38–39) needs to find her daughter or the earth will remain barren.

Central to many mythologies is the idea that the gods or ancestors taught the crafts and skills that enable humankind to survive. Therefore, the most everyday acts are infused with mythical power. When, for instance, the South American peoples of the Orinoco river, such as the Warao (see pages 122–123), weave their intricate baskets and re-tell the origin stories symbolized by each basket pattern, they are giving visible form to the invisible world of myth.

Rain-making is a function of the kachina spirits of the American southwest. These spirit beings are represented in ceremonies by masked dancers (kachina doll, right), who summon the cloud fathers to come and bring rain.

The daily life of the Warao (background, see pages 122–123) of Venezuela is entwined with their myths, for their canoes are alive with the spirit of Dauarani, the mother of the forest. When a boat-maker wishes to cut down a tree to make a canoe, he must gain the consent of the female tree spirit to be felled. Then he must protect her with sacred chants from the spirit jaguar, which comes in the night to jeer at the tree maiden, whose body is being 'eaten' by the axes of men.

MYTH AND GEOGRAPHY

The homeland of the Wishram peoples on the lower Columbia river in Oregon and Washington, USA, is watched over by a brooding face carved into a large block of volcanic rock (above). It depicts Tsagiglalal, the goddess who watches all who are coming or going. In the creation-time, before the trickster Coyote came upriver and changed things, she was chief of all those who lived in that area. But Coyote turned her into a rock, and told her to keep watch over the Wishram.

Just as societies and cultures are shaped by the geography of the land a people inhabits, so too are mythologies. For example, the myths of the Warao (see pages 122–123) of the Orinoco delta, South America, portray the world as a flat disc surrounded by water. This is because the Warao live at sea level and see the land as a flat strip between the water and the sky.

LAND SHAPING MYTH

Peoples such as the Warao (see page 19) are perfectly attuned to the environment in which they live. Their myths are on one level exciting stories about sacred beings in the creation-time, and on another are a detailed guide to the delicately balanced ecology of the Warao world.

This intimate interweaving of mythology and geography is obviously more apparent among a people such as the Warao, whose territory is highly specialized and very precisely bounded. An example from a much more complex society might be that of ancient Egypt, where their mythology was shaped by the way the annual flooding of the River Nile fertilized a narrow strip of land in the Egyptian desert.

The idea of a magical early race, the First People, who could take human or animal form, and who were transformed in various ways on the arrival of the present-day humans, the Real People, exists in all native American mythology, but especially in California. There, the doings of the First People are still celebrated today in myths and ceremonies. The First People themselves are still powerfully present in the landscape, having transformed themselves into animals, birds, rocks, landmarks or spirits.

In Egyptian mythology, the sacred Benu bird flew across the primeval ocean to a rocky mound which poked above the surface, alighted, and let out a harsh cry which called the world into being. This mound provided the model for the pyramids in which the mummies of the pharaohs were buried.

A LIVING COUNTRY

In southern Africa, the mythology of the San people is concerned with the doings of the animal-people of the Early Race. Myths of this type make the landscape, and all that lives in it, sacred. Nowhere is this more evident than in Australia, where every feature of the landscape testifies to the presence of the Aboriginal ancestral beings of the Dreaming, the creation-time (see pages 134–135). The Dreaming songs interconnect and turn the whole of Australia into a living body, with the giant sandstone monolith of Uluru (main image) at its heart.

In Mesopotamia, the gods were called to witness royal gifts of land. The symbols of the divine witnesses were engraved at the top of kudurrus, boundary stones, copies of which were erected on the land itself and in the temples of the gods. The text on this stone calls down the wrath of the gods on those who break the agreements.

Aboriginal sacred places such as Uluru (above) are storehouses of magical energy akin to the life force, known as djang, which is re-charged by ritual activity. The Aboriginal peoples believe that Uluru was built in the Dreaming by two boys playing in the mud after rain. It was the site of a great battle in the Dreaming between two warring groups of snake-people, the Kuniya and the Liru.

MYTH AND THE STARS

The dance of the stars in the night sky and the slow revolution of the planets have inspired humankind. It is by observing the sun, the moon and the stars that we measure time. Early peoples read in the stars a narrative of change, disaster and renewal that defined their world.

Each evening, as the sun reached the westernmost peak of Mount Manu, the Egyptian sky goddess Nut (left) swallowed it. Each morning, she gave birth to the sun once more in the east.

STAR CHILDREN

In ancient Egyptian mythology, the stars were the children of Nut, the sky, and Geb, the dry land. After the birth of the stars, Nut's father cursed her so that she would never again give birth in any month of the year. But Nut gambled with Thoth, the moon god and reckoner of time, and won from him five extra days, to be added to the original 12 lunar months of 30 days each. In these days, she gave birth to her children, Osiris (see pages 144–145), Blind Horus, Seth, Isis (see page 50) and Nepthys.

Without the addition of a leap day every four years, the Egyptian calendar of 365 days gradually slipped out of step with the true year. The two coincided only once every 1,460 years, a period of mystical significance for the ancient Egyptian priesthood.

The Nebra sky disc was probably used as a calendar for planting and harvesting crops. It depicts the sun and a crescent moon, the stars, two arcs (only one is still gilded) that define the summer and winter solstices, and a golden ship (bottom of the main image).

Mesoamerican civilizations, such as the Aztecs and the Maya, meshed both a 260-day and a 365-day cycle in the 'calendar round' which took 52 years to complete (Aztec calendar stone showing the Five Ages of the world, left). Some highland Maya today still observe this cycle.

An old sky

The importance of astronomy to early cultures is emphasized by a remarkable Bronze Age object excavated on the top of Mittelberg mountain, Germany. This is the Nebra sky disc (main image), which shows the night sky from the Mittelberg as it was around 1600BCE, and features a golden ship that is probably the sky boat in which the sun was believed to travel.

The Incas foresaw their own downfall in the stars. Believing that the sun and the stars were at war, they attempted to tie them together, by rituals at sites such as the hitching-post of the sun at Machu Picchu, Peru. The Incas pleaded with their supreme god Viracocha (right), 'May the world not turn over'.

THE MEANING OF MYTHS

Myths evolve over time, and each re-telling or re-enactment of a myth may be subtly different from any previous one. It is a mistake to think of them as fixed, for one of the strengths of myth is its flexibility. This is especially true when considering what a particular myth means. Myths are rich in meaning, and can be interpreted in many different ways.

In the mythology of ancient Persia, the work of the creator Ahura Mazda (above) was marred by the destroyer Angra Mainya. So Ahura Mazda trapped Angra Mainya inside creation. When time comes to an end Angra Mainya will be cast out of creation and a new, unsullied world will come into being.

The Aztec civilization of Mexico was in part brought down because its last ruler, Montezuma, believed in Aztec myths. Shortly before the Spanish conquistadors arrived in 1519, the kingdom was full of dire prophecies. Some hunters brought a bird to the king with a mirror in its head, in which the heavens could be seen. When Montezuma looked in it, all he saw was a host of armed men. The handful of Spanish adventurers under Hernán Cortés overthrew the Aztecs easily because Montezuma believed Cortés to be the god Quetzalcoatl, returned from across the ocean to reclaim his kingdom (see pages 116–117).

Prince Rama was born for the specific purpose of defeating the evil demon Ravana. Rama was half-human and half-god, having half of the divine essence of Vishnu, the preserver. The Hindu myth of Rama's quest to rescue his wife Sita from the evil clutches of Ravana (left) is one of the most widespread and best-loved stories in the world (see pages 78–79).

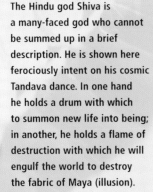

The Hindu god Shiva is a many-faced god who cannot be summed up in a brief description. He is shown here ferociously intent on his cosmic Tandava dance. In one hand he holds a drum with which to summon new life into being; in another, he holds a flame of destruction with which he will engulf the world to destroy the fabric of Maya (illusion).

The Mesopotamian goddess Inanna (right, see pages 68–69) was revered by the Sumerians as the queen of heaven and earth. At the heart of her myth is her suffering in the underworld in her bid to wrest the secrets of life and death from her sister Ereshkigal. The myths of this powerful goddess of love and war transferred from one culture to another, subtly changing each time. The Babylonians called her Ishtar; the Canaanites called her Anath or Astarte.

Providing answers

Myths are not fixed truths, but flexible representations of the truth. They try to provide answers to the basic questions of existence; for instance, to explain why the world is so full of suffering. Through stories, poems, songs and symbols, myths from around the world explore the unfathomable mysteries of life and death.

Many mythologies take a dualistic view, seeing the world as ruled by opposing deities of good and evil. In other mythologies, the powers of creation and destruction may be combined in a single god. For instance, in Hindu belief, the god Shiva (see pages 76–77) is responsible as Mahakala for both the creation and destruction of all things.

The all-encompassing nature of myth can be encapsulated in a single object such as the Sacred Pole of the Omaha Nation of the North American plains. Called the Venerable Man, this pole was central to the ceremonies and beliefs of the Omaha. The pole was regarded and treated as a human being, and revered as provider and protector. The Venerable Man, it was said, 'held the tribe together'. Myths are alive in just the same way as the Venerable Man. They draw together strands of meaning and memory.

ATLANTIC OCEAN

ICELAND

Ymir

Loki

N

W E

S

(SCANDINAVIA)

NORWAY

SWEDEN

Väinämöinen FINLAND

Balder

Odin

SCOTLAND

(UNITED KINGDOM)

Dagda

REPUBLIC OF IRELAND

WALES

ENGLAND

DENMARK

GERMANY

EASTERN EUROPE

Willendorf Venus

FRANCE

SPAIN

Vesta

Flora

Cybele

Romulus & Remus

ITALY

Zeus

Apollo

GREECE

Athena

Trojan horse

Demeter

Minotaur

Snake goddess

CRETE

AFRICA

EUROPE

Europe has had successive waves of immigration by different peoples. The Celts, for instance, were pushed to the western fringes, including Ireland, where the most complete versions of Celtic myths have been recorded. But it is the ancient civilizations of Greece and Rome that have left the greatest wealth of myth, whose influences stretch back into the Bronze Age.

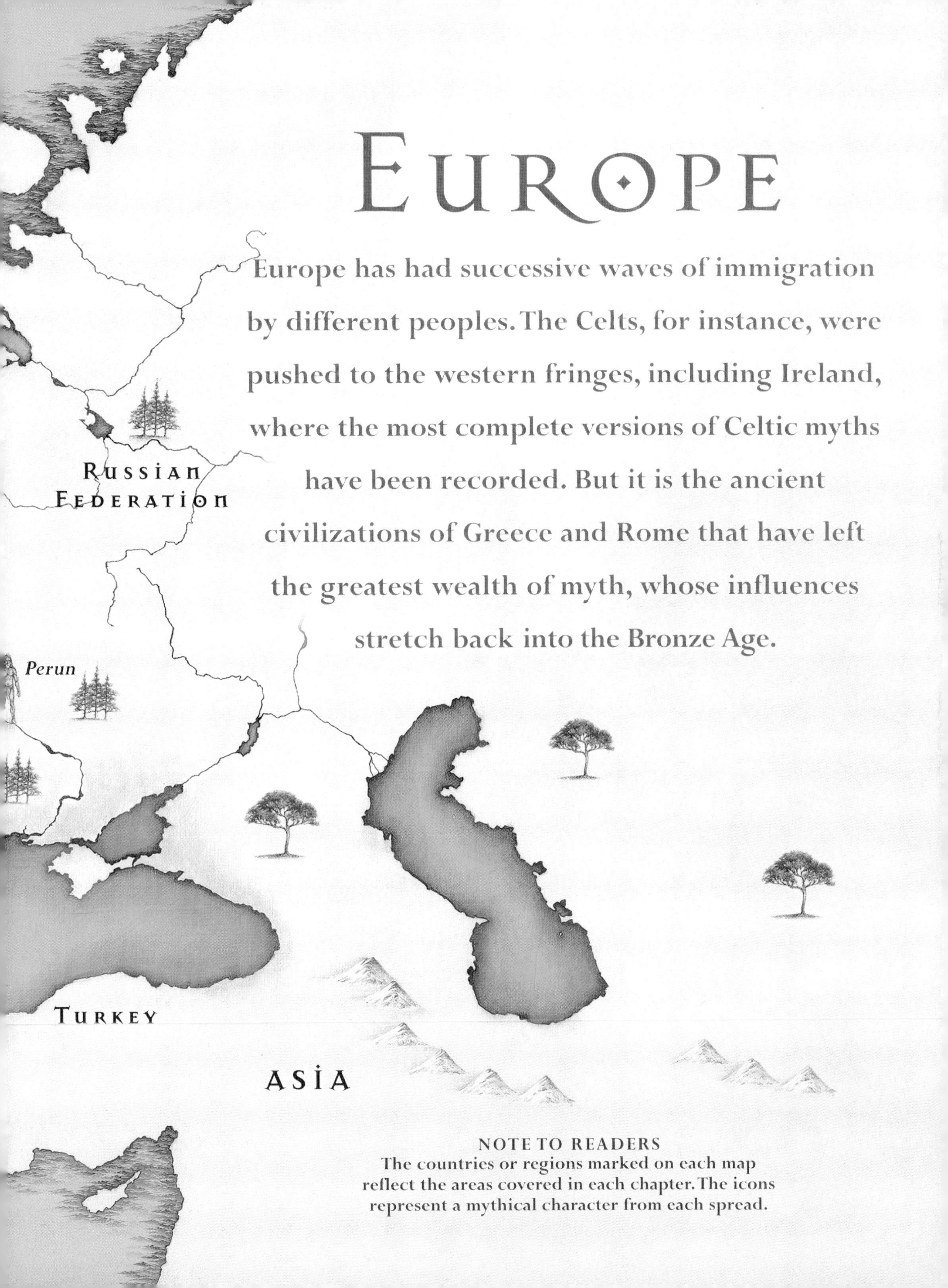

RUSSIAN
FEDERATION

Perun

TURKEY

ASIA

NOTE TO READERS
The countries or regions marked on each map
reflect the areas covered in each chapter. The icons
represent a mythical character from each spread.

Lost in Time

uch of the world's mythology has vanished leaving scarcely a trace. The peoples of prehistoric Europe, for instance, left no written record of their myths. But they did leave remarkable cave paintings that offer a glimpse into their beliefs. However, archaeological evidence alone cannot reconstruct these lost myths.

Palaeolithic cave paintings – made with charcoal from burned wood or bone, and red and yellow ochre from iron oxide – usually show hunting scenes, depicting animals such as bison (above), deer and horses. The human figures are often portrayed with animal features such as horns and tails. These half-human, half-animal figures almost certainly represent Ice Age shamans, whose magical rites were relied on to ensure success in the hunt.

Ice Age cave paintings

The Palaeolithic people of the Ice Age, from around 38000 to 8000BCE, left very expressive and beautiful rock art in caves across Europe. Evidence such as this allows us to try to reconstruct the mythological world of the first Europeans. Other clues come from strange symbols inscribed on rocks; treasures cast away at sacred sites or buried in graves; and images of gods and goddesses whose names we will never know.

Many Stone Age figures show a female deity, sometimes with bird or snake characteristics. This bird goddess or snake goddess (see pages 30–31), often decorated with meander (wavy) patterns to suggest rain, is the goddess of the water and the air. That she was worshipped as the great mother is suggested by figurines of her holding a baby (left). There may have been a connection in Stone Age belief between the rain that nurtures the crops and the milk that nurtures infants.

STONE AGE STATUES

Neolithic people living in Europe from around 7000BCE, after the end of the Ice Age, inherited many of the thought patterns of their predecessors, but added other elements to their myths and rituals to reflect the new importance of agriculture alongside hunting and gathering. Like their Ice Age ancestors, these Stone Age people carved stone images of gods and goddesses. They also fashioned them from clay.

Elements of Stone Age mythology underly Bronze Age myths. But there is also an increasing emphasis on a powerful male sky god, who is shown in Scandinavian rock engravings (right) brandishing an axe or hammer, perhaps as a forerunner of the Viking god Thor (see pages 56–57).

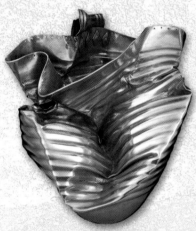

This Bronze Age gold cup was found at Ringlemere in East Sussex, England, in 2001. It dates from 1700–1500BCE. Although badly crushed, perhaps by a plough, it shows the skills of Bronze Age craftsmen. The cup was buried with its owner, so that he could drink from it in the afterlife.

Sun worship was a new development in the Bronze Age, perhaps because the sun represents fire, which is essential for metalworking. Cult objects (example, right), such as the glorious Chariot of the Sun from the 14th century BCE, found in Trundholm, Denmark, provide evidence for this theory. The Chariot of the Sun is a bronze horse pulling a wheeled gold sun disc, and probably represents the sun god crossing the sky. Both the wheel and the chariot were new technologies in the Bronze Age, unknown to previous cultures.

BRONZE AGE ADVANCES

The European Bronze Age, which began around 2500BCE, saw a profound leap in human civilization. Bronze weapons and tools led to an extraordinary growth in craftsmanship, trade and all aspects of culture, including religion and mythology. The start of the Bronze Age is roughly the same date as the founding of the first city of Troy (see pages 42–43), and of the great pre-Greek cultures, such as Minoan Crete (see pages 32–33). And with all its other advances, the Bronze Age also brought Europe into the age of the written word.

It is from these now-lost myths and cults of the Bronze Age that the great European mythologies of the Greeks, the Romans, the Scandinavians and the Celts were formed.

THE DIVINE CHILD

The classical civilization of ancient Greece was the creation of the Dorian people who invaded Greece around 1100BCE. They supplanted an earlier civilization in the Aegean, which was centred on the island of Crete. This earlier civilization is often called Minoan, after King Minos of Crete (see pages 32–33). The early Minoans settled in Crete in the late Stone Age — archaeologists believe they came from western Asia.

Zeus was worshipped on Crete both as a divine child and as a kouros, a beardless youth, but many later statues portrayed him as an older man with a beard.

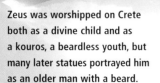

Minoan Crete was famous for its honey. As in other parts of Europe, the mother goddess was worshipped in bee form (pendant, right) as a goddess of regeneration. The birthplace of Zeus, her son, was a sacred cave of bees, which no man or god might enter. When four men dared to try to steal the honey, Zeus turned them into birds.

THE LOST CITY OF ATLANTIS

The great palace of Knossos, in Crete, was first excavated by the archaeologist Sir Arthur Evans (1851–1941) at the beginning of the 20th century CE. People were so excited by his finds that many thought he had discovered the lost city of Atlantis. Today, some scholars still believe that Atlantis was part of the Minoan civilization, although they think it was actually the island of Santorini, which was devastated by an earthquake around 1450BCE.

BUSY BEES

As her Titan husband Kronos had swallowed each of his children as soon as they were born, the mother goddess Rhea hid her last son, Zeus, from him. She then tricked Kronos into swallowing a stone instead of his son.

Rhea gave birth in secret on Mount Dikte, and the new-born god was nourished with the honey of the sacred bees which lived in the cave. He was then given into the care of two nymphs, the daughters of Melisseus, the honey-man.

This clay disc inscribed with a spiral of hieroglyphs was found in the palace of Phaestos in 1903. No one has been able to decipher it, but it is thought to be a hymn to the great mother goddess, who was worshipped across Crete.

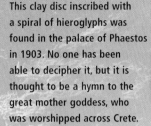

The mother goddess of Minoan Crete is evidently related to the snake goddess (shown here with a musician) who was worshipped throughout the civilizations of early Europe. This goddess is often signified by a meander pattern, symbolizing her cosmic rain (see page 28). The meander is also the basic constituent of the maze, or labyrinth, and on Crete the mother goddess was worshipped as the mistress of the labyrinth.

Minoan Crete

Before the earthquake, Santorini, which was colonized by the Minoans around 3000BCE, was a round island, just as Atlantis was described; today it is a mere horseshoe. Whether this was the origin of the Atlantis myth or not, the tsunami from the huge earthquake at Santorini almost certainly devastated Minoan Crete, and weakened its civilization to the point where the Dorian Greek invaders could conquer it.

The Minoans worshipped a great mother goddess, who may have been called Rhea, and had a myth about her giving birth to a son in the Diktian cave at Psychró, Crete. The Dorian Greeks gave this son the name of their own supreme god, Zeus. But it may be that originally the divine infant was the god of indestructible life, Dionysos, who in his Minoan form seems to have taken some of the qualities of Zeus.

It is Dionysos whose divine birth in the underworld was celebrated in the religious Mysteries of Eleusis (see pages 38–39). The rites, which were conducted in the strictest secrecy in Eleusis, had been openly celebrated at Knossos from the earliest times.

31

A DEADLY MAZE

The legends of Minoan Crete have
come down to us through Greek
mythology. To the ancient Greeks,
the half-man, half-bull Minotaur
was simply a monster, to be slain
by the Athenian hero Theseus
(see page 37). But to the Minoans,
the Minotaur had a divine nature,
and the story of its ritual sacrifice
carried a profound message of rebirth.

This figure of a young Minoan man,
from a much-restored fresco at the
palace of King Minos at Knossos, is
known as the Priest-King or Prince
of the Lilies. Other palace frescoes
show young men and women
leaping over bulls in a ritual
display of bravery and athleticism.

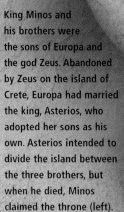

King Minos and
his brothers were
the sons of Europa and
the god Zeus. Abandoned
by Zeus on the island of
Crete, Europa had married
the king, Asterios, who
adopted her sons as his
own. Asterios intended to
divide the island between
the three brothers, but
when he died, Minos
claimed the throne (left).

SHADOW OF THE KING

The name Minotaur simply means 'bull of
Minos'. It is likely that the name Minos was
actually a Minoan word for king, as Menes
was for the early Egyptian pharaohs. And
as with the pharaohs, the symbol of the
king's strength and divinity was the bull.
The Minotaur is a kind of a shadow or symbol
of the king, and was even given a king's
name, Asterios, which means 'star'. Some early
depictions of the Minotaur's labyrinth show
a star, not a monster, at the heart of the maze.

The labyrinth was named after the Minoan
double-headed ritual axe, known as the labrys.

Such an axe may have been
used to sacrifice a bull in the
lost Minoan religious mysteries.

The pattern of the labyrinth,
found on Minoan vases, coins and
frescoes, is a kind of map of the route
to the underworld. Its winding maze
reflects the steps of ritual dances to the
mother goddess (see page 31). Homer
(c.700BCE) wrote in his epic, *The Iliad*,
about 'the dancing floor', which was built
in Knossos for 'lovely-haired Ariadne'. Ariadne
was the daughter of King Minos of Crete.

A FORGOTTEN PROMISE

In revenge for the death of his son Androgeos, King Minos attacked Athens and reduced the city to famine and plague. King Aigeus of Athens admitted defeat and agreed to send a tribute of seven boys and seven girls every nine years, as food for King Minos' Minotaur. The youths to be sacrificed were chosen by drawing lots. King Aigeus was shocked when his own heir, the hero Theseus, was chosen.

The ships carrying the victims to Crete hoisted black sails in mourning, but Theseus asked the king to give him a white sail as well, promising that he would raise it if he returned. Theseus did defeat the Minotaur, but he forgot his promise. King Aigeus saw the black sail and threw himself into the sea and drowned.

To prove his claim to the throne, Minos stood on the beach and asked Poseidon, the sea god, to send him a great bull from the sea, to sacrifice to the god. Immediately a great bull arose from the depths. But Minos did not sacrifice it; instead he killed a lesser animal. Poseidon was so insulted that he made Minos' wife, Pasiphae, fall in love with the bull, and bear it a child, the Minotaur, a monstrous creature with the head of a bull but the body of a man.

SLAYING THE BEAST

Ariadne, the daughter of King Minos and Queen Pasiphae, was the mistress of the labyrinth. When Theseus arrived in Crete, Ariadne fell in love with him. She asked the craftsman Daidalos, who had designed the labyrinth in which the Minotaur was confined, to help her guide Theseus through the maze. Daidalos gave her a reel of thread, telling her to tie it to the door of the labyrinth, unwind it on the way to the centre, and then rewind it to retrace the route. Ariadne gave the thread to Theseus, having first won his promise to take her with him to Athens and to marry her.

Theseus entered the labyrinth and tracked the Minotaur to his lair at the heart of the maze. They fought, and Theseus slew the beast with his bare hands. He then followed the thread to find his way out of the maze.

On the way home, Theseus, who did not love Ariadne, abandoned her on the island of Naxos, and went on his way.

GODS OF OLYMPUS

The chief god of the ancient Greeks was Zeus (see pages 30–31), a sky god whose weapon was the thunderbolt. The Greek gods were thought to live in a heavenly realm in the sky above the summit of the highest mountain in Greece, Mount Olympus. From the realm of Olympus, the gods watched over the world, helping or hindering mortals according to their whims.

The myth in which Zeus and the Olympian gods (above) destroy the power of the tyrannical Titans is presented as a war for freedom. The concept of eleutheria (freedom) was central to the Greeks. When praying, they stood erect. To bow would be to behave like a slave.

THE SUPREME GOD

Zeus became the supreme god because he rescued his brothers and sisters after they had been swallowed by their father, the Titan Kronos. Zeus then led his siblings in the war against the Titans, who were the children of Gaia, the earth, and Ouranos, the sky.

Poseidon was the god of the sea. When angered, he caused storms at sea and earthquakes on land. Poseidon once conspired with Hera, Athena and Apollo to depose Zeus as king of the gods, but Zeus was freed from his chains by Briareos, one of the Hundred-Handed Giants whose task was to guard the Titans in Tartaros.

THE THREE REALMS

Zeus was the youngest of the six children of Kronos and Rhea, so his position as their ruler was a delicate one. According to one myth, Zeus and his brothers cast lots to divide the world between them. Zeus became ruler of the heavens, Poseidon of the sea, and Hades of the underworld. Although the supremacy of Zeus is rarely challenged in Greek myths, he is never shown as interfering in the realms of Poseidon and Hades.

An unfaithful husband

Zeus himself shared power with his wife Hera, the goddess of marriage. She bore him four children: Ares, the god of war; Hebe, the goddess of youth; Eileithuia, the goddess of childbirth; and Hephaistos, the blacksmith god.

But these are by no means all of Zeus's children. Others, including goddesses and gods such as Athena (see pages 36–37) and Apollo (see pages 40–41), and heroes such as Herakles (see page 37), were fathered with goddesses, nymphs and mortal women. Many of the myths featuring Hera concentrate on her jealousy over Zeus's love affairs.

According to mythology, Hera was once so infuriated by her husband's unfaithfulness that she left him. So Zeus made a wooden statue of a woman, and exhibited this, veiled, as his new wife. Hera was so jealous she rushed to attack her rival. When she removed the veil and realized it was a statue, she laughed so much she forgot to be angry.

The most important conflict between Zeus and Hera was in the Trojan War (see pages 42–43), in which, against Zeus's orders, Hera helped the Greeks to win the war.

Hades (shown here with his wife Persephone, see pages 38–39) ruled the world of the dead, which was also called Hades. There, the majority of the dead lived a listless existence on the featureless Plain of Asphodel. Only a lucky few enjoyed the bliss of the Elysian fields, while others suffered everlasting torment in Tartaros. Hades was sometimes called 'Zeus of the underworld'.

A titanic battle

When the youngest of the Titans, Kronos, assumed power, he imprisoned his powerful brothers, the three Hundred-Handed Giants and the three one-eyed Kyklopes, under the earth. Because it was prophesied that Kronos would be overthrown by his child, whenever his wife Rhea gave birth he swallowed the baby: first Hestia, then Demeter, Hera, Hades and Poseidon. So Rhea fled to Crete to give birth to Zeus*, and afterwards wrapped a stone in swaddling cloth, and tricked Kronos into swallowing this instead of Zeus. When Zeus was older, he sought the aid of his cousin Metis, who gave Kronos a drug that made him vomit up the other children. Zeus then enlisted them in a war against Kronos and the other Titans. He also freed the Hundred-Handers and the Kyklopes, who forged the thunderbolts with which Zeus overthrew the Titans. Zeus cast the Titans into Tartaros – which is as far below the earth as heaven is above – where they will be guarded until the end of time.

* Zeus (above)

35

THE CITY GUARDIAN

The Greek word polis is usually translated as 'city-state'. The Greek city-states, such as Athens, bound their citizens together in a unity of purpose and belief that was powered by mythology and ritual. Each city-state had its presiding god or goddess: Athena in Athens, Apollo (see pages 40–41) in Delphi, Poseidon in Corinth, Hera in Argos, and so on. In many ways, the Greek myths had the most resonance and meaning at the level of the city-state, where they entwined with the daily lives of the ancient Greeks.

PLATO'S DREAM

The Greek philosopher Plato (427–348BCE) said that the ideal city should have 5,000 male citizens, plus families and slaves. Plato's idea of the perfect city was shaped by his negative experience of Athens, his home city. In Plato's time, Athens had over 40,000 citizens – too many for each citizen to be able to know all the others by sight, as Plato's pupil Aristotle (384–322BCE) said they should.

Across Greece, Athena (above) was worshipped as the goddess of war and wisdom, but in Athens she was Athena Polias, or Athena, guardian of the city. According to mythology, at the founding of the city, Athena and Poseidon vied for the position of guardian. The citizens agreed to accept the god who gave them the most useful gift. Poseidon struck the ground and a spring emerged. Athena made an olive tree grow, and her gift was preferred, for Poseidon's spring was of salty seawater.

ATHENA'S FESTIVAL

The Athenians credited the forging of Athens into a single dominant city-state to the hero Theseus (see pages 32–33). As king of Athens, Theseus redefined the city's worship of Athena in the Great Panathenaia Festival as something that included not just the citizens of Athens, but all other Greek citizens as well.

This festival was held once every four years at the end of July, and included processions, horse races, musical and athletic contests, as well as religious rituals. During the festival, the 12m-high statue of Athena, in the Parthenon, was dressed in a new robe woven by the women of the city. This robe was embroidered with mythological scenes celebrating the goddess. The festival itself was depicted by a sculpted frieze on the walls of the Parthenon. This frieze is now known as the Elgin Marbles and housed in the British Museum, England.

The centre of Athena's worship was the Parthenon temple (left) on the Akropolis, which was built around 447BCE. There is also a smaller temple to Athena Nike, the goddess of victory. It was from this temple that King Aigeus threw himself into the sea, when he mistakenly thought that Theseus, his son, had been killed by the Minotaur (see page 33).

THESEUS FORGETS

Theseus was the foremost hero of Athens, and its greatest king. On his way to Athens, to claim his birthright as the son of King Aigeus, Theseus performed deeds of valour, culminating in his voyage to Crete to slay the Minotaur.

But the most daring of Theseus's exploits was his search for a new wife. When Theseus and his friend Peirithoos became widowers, they decided that they should marry daughters of Zeus.

First of all, Theseus abducted Helen of Sparta, whose beauty was later to spark the Trojan War. He and Peirithoos then descended to the underworld to capture the goddess Persephone. Persephone's husband, the god Hades, received them politely, and asked them to sit down. They did so, and found that their flesh had stuck to the Chairs of Forgetfulness, which made them lose their memories. They remained trapped until Herakles arrived to capture the watchdog of the underworld, Kerberos. Recognizing his cousin, Herakles wrenched Theseus free; but he could not free Peirithoos, so they had to leave him in eternal torment.

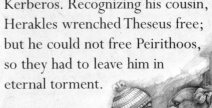

DEMETER'S FURY

The myth of Demeter and Persephone lies behind the most important religious rites of ancient Greece, the Mysteries of Eleusis. Those initiated into the Mysteries experienced a profound revelation of a new life after death. They were forbidden to betray the secrets of the Mysteries to any outsider, and even today the exact nature of the rituals is still unclear. But we know that initiates were shown an ear of corn – perhaps one that seemed to have grown magically from seed before their very eyes.

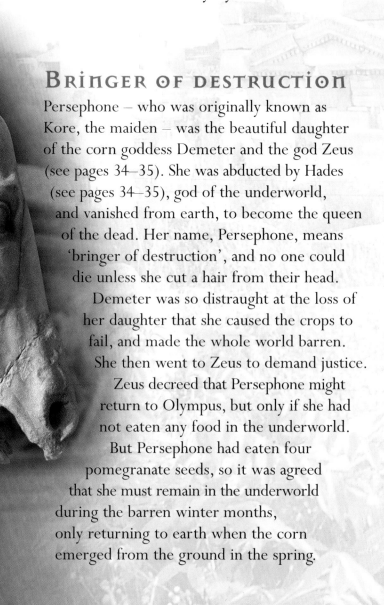

BRINGER OF DESTRUCTION

Persephone – who was originally known as Kore, the maiden – was the beautiful daughter of the corn goddess Demeter and the god Zeus (see pages 34–35). She was abducted by Hades (see pages 34–35), god of the underworld, and vanished from earth, to become the queen of the dead. Her name, Persephone, means 'bringer of destruction', and no one could die unless she cut a hair from their head.

Demeter was so distraught at the loss of her daughter that she caused the crops to fail, and made the whole world barren. She then went to Zeus to demand justice. Zeus decreed that Persephone might return to Olympus, but only if she had not eaten any food in the underworld. But Persephone had eaten four pomegranate seeds, so it was agreed that she must remain in the underworld during the barren winter months, only returning to earth when the corn emerged from the ground in the spring.

Demeter is sometimes shown with a mare's head, recalling a myth in which she and Poseidon (see page 34) turned into horses. They had a daughter, the Mistress, who was the focus of the Mysteries of Arcadia.

Favoured child

For nine days and nights, Demeter* searched the underworld in vain for her missing daughter. On the tenth day, she discovered that it was Hades who had stolen Persephone. Demeter was so angry she refused to return to Olympus. Shunning the other gods, she pretended to be a mortal woman, and took service as a nursemaid in the king's household at Eleusis. She took charge of the king's baby, Triptolemos**, anointing him with ambrosia, the food of the gods, by day, and at night placing him in the burning embers of the fire. Her aim was to make the child immortal, but she was discovered by the infant's mother, who screamed and spoiled Demeter's plan.

However, the goddess still showed the child special favour. She gave Triptolemos a chariot drawn by winged dragons, and a supply of corn, which he sowed over the whole world as he was carried along in the sky.

* Demeter (far left)
** Triptolemos (centre)

A vision of life

According to mythology, when Demeter restored fertility to the world, she also taught humankind the rites of the Mysteries which were to be celebrated in her honour. These rites, the people of Eleusis believed, held the whole human race together. They were therefore open to slaves and Greek-speaking foreigners as well as Greek citizens, and to women as well as men.

Each year, initiates prepared and purified themselves to receive a revelation of life after death. In a drugged state, they were shown many visions in flashes of light, culminating in the display of a magical ear of corn.

The Mysteries of Eleusis were observed for 2,000 years, but came to an end in CE396 when the holy shrine of Demeter was sacked by Alaric, king of the Goths (ruled from CE394 to 410). However, the ancient Greeks of Eleusis (modern Elefsina) continued to worship their goddess (right, with the sacred objects known as the cista mystica) as Saint Demetra, even after they had converted to Christianity.

Another key revelation was that in the underworld Persephone had given birth in fire to a divine child, Brimos, the strong one. This name seems to refer to Dionysos (see page 31), the god of indestructible life.

39

THE POWER OF PROPHECY

When the Titan Kronos vomited up the stone he had swallowed believing it to be the baby Zeus (see pages 30–31), the stone landed at Delphi in central Greece, where it was revered as the Omphalos Stone, the navel of the world. However, the great temple at Delphi was not dedicated to Zeus, but to his son Apollo, the god of prophecy, music and archery.

A few days after he was born, Apollo was fully grown, having been fed on ambrosia by the goddess Themis, who was the mother of the Hours and the Fates, and could foresee the future.

The ancient temple of Apollo at Delphi was burned down in 548BCE, and replaced with one even more magnificent. Above the doorway were inscribed the words 'Know thyself', as a warning to those questioning the Pythia to seek wisdom within. Inside the temple was the Omphalos Stone (right), one of the holiest objects in Delphi.

THE PYTHIA

According to mythology, when Apollo came to Delphi, he found a cleft in the rock guarded by the Python, the snake-daughter of the earth goddess Gaia. He shot the serpent with his bow and arrow, and founded his shrine, with an oracular priestess named the Pythia. People came from all over Greece to seek advice on the future from the Pythia.

The Pythia prophesied in an underground chamber. Modern research has shown that this chamber beneath Apollo's temple lies above two intersecting fault lines in the limestone rocks. In the 1st century CE, the writer Plutarch (c.CE45–125), who was a member of the college of priests at Delphi, noted that this chamber was filled with a sweet-smelling gas. This was caused by ethylene vapours seeping through fissures into the chamber, to induce a trance in which the Pythia was able to utter prophecies.

The Greeks held in high regard the oracle of the Egyptian god Amun (see pages 142–143), also called Horned Ammon, who lived in an oasis in the Libyan desert, served by over 100 priests. This shrine was visited, for instance, by Alexander the Great (356–323BCE) after his conquest of Egypt in 332BCE. It was said that the oracle recognized Alexander (above) as the 'son of Amun', thus legitimizing his rule.

THE LAWS OF SPARTA

The laws of Sparta were said to have been revealed to the Spartan leader Lykourgos (c.7th century BCE) by the oracle at Delphi. These rigid laws, devised around 600BCE, trained Sparta's citizens to devote themselves selflessly to the common good. They remained unchanged for centuries, during which time the Spartans won a reputation for courage, dutifulness and endurance. All Spartan boys and girls underwent tough physical training, because the Spartan people were soldiers; any other work was done by the Helots, their slaves.

AN EXPENSIVE READ

The ancient Greeks believed firmly in the power of prophecy, and the oracle at Delphi was only one of many oracular shrines. Another famous oracle was that of Zeus at Dodona, Greece. Here, the prophecies of the god were interpreted by priests from the sounds made by the spring which rose from the roots of a sacred oak tree, and from the rustling of the leaves.

Most oracles had their own priestess, or sibyl. The most famous of these was the sibyl of Cumae. She owned nine books of prophecies, which she offered to sell to Tarquinius Superbus (c.534–510BCE), the last king of Rome, at a very high price. When he refused, she burned three of the books, and offered the remaining six to him again, but at the same price as before. He refused again, and she burned three more books. Eventually, Tarquinius bought the last three books for the same price that he had originally been offered for all nine! They became one of the great treasures of Rome, until they were destroyed when the capitol was burned in 83BCE.

ETERNAL LIFE

When the sibyl of Cumae was still young and beautiful, Apollo fell in love with her. Hoping to win her love, he offered her whatever she wanted. The sibyl pointed to a heap of dust on the floor of her cave, and said, 'Give me as many years of life as there are grains of dust in that pile.' Apollo granted her request, but the haughty young woman then rejected his advances. However, the sibyl had forgotten to ask for eternal youth, and as the centuries passed she withered away, until she was so tiny and shrunken that she ended her days hung up in a jar, like an insect. When some children saw her then, and asked the sibyl what she wanted, she answered, 'I want to die.'

Fighting for Helen

The epic tale of the Trojan War is told in *The Iliad* (see page 32), which was composed by Homer in the 8th century BCE. Homer blends myth and history in his account of the siege and destruction of the city of Troy, also called Ilium, in the 13th century BCE. At this time, the Minoan civilization still held sway in ancient Greece, before the Dorian invasion around 1100BCE, from which classical Greece emerged. So for Homer, the Achaian heroes of the Trojan War were figures from the dim past, not his contemporary world.

Helen was the daughter of Zeus and Leda. Her brothers were Kastor and Polydeukes, the Dioskouroi, the heavenly twins, who were worshipped as Castor and Pollux by the Romans. Helen's brothers rescued her from the Athenian king Theseus (see pages 32–33, 37).

Homer's epic concentrates on the final year of the siege of Troy, when Achilles killed Hektor, the prince of Troy. As he died, Hektor declared that Achilles would be slain by Paris. Achilles was almost invulnerable to weapons, for his mother dipped him as a baby in the River Styx, which ran through the underworld. She held him by one heel, leaving just that one point vulnerable. Paris fired an arrow into the exact spot, and killed him. After the death of Achilles, Aias and Odysseus contested for Achilles' divine armour (left); Odysseus won.

Beautiful Helen

The cause of the great war between the Achaians and the Trojans was a quarrel over the most beautiful woman in the world, Helen. She was a Spartan princess, who was given in marriage to Menelaos, the king of Sparta; her sister, Klytaimestra, was already married to Menelaos' brother, Agamemnon, the king of Mycenae.

Helen was stolen away from Menelaos by Paris, the son of Priam, the king of Troy. Helen was the reward offered to Paris by Aphrodite, the goddess of love, in return for choosing her in a beauty contest between three goddesses: Aphrodite, Athena and Hera, who all competed for a golden apple inscribed 'for the fairest', with Paris as the judge.

Under the leadership of King Agamemnon, the Achaians sailed to Troy with a great fleet, and laid siege to the city in order to get Helen back. Their greatest warrior was the legendary Achilles. The Achaians were also aided by the goddesses Athena and Hera, whose pride had been wounded by Paris's choice of Aphrodite.

THERE IS NO ONE HERE

After the fall of Troy, the Achaian heroes suffered many tragedies because they had offended one or other of the gods. Odysseus' troubles began when he landed his ships on the island of the three one-eyed giants, the Kyklopes. Odysseus and his men hoped that one of the Kyklopes, Polyphemos, would welcome them as guests, but instead he imprisoned them in his cave, and began to eat the men.

In order to escape, Odysseus tricked Polyphemos into drinking some strong wine, which made him woozy. Odysseus then said that his name was Outis, which means 'no one'. While Polyphemos was in a drunken stupor, Odysseus and his men heated a wooden stake in the fire until it was red hot, and then plunged it into the giant's single eye. When Polyphemos screamed for help, he told his fellow Kyklopes that 'no one' was hurting him, so they did not come to his aid. Odysseus and his remaining men escaped from the cave. But as he left, Odysseus taunted the blinded Polyphemos, and told him his real name. As a result, Polyphemos's father, Poseidon, persecuted Odysseus for ten long years, and killed all his companions.

THE WINNING SIDE

The siege of Troy lasted for ten years. The war was finally brought to an end by the cunning of Odysseus, the prince of Ithaka, who instructed the Achaians to build a large wooden horse.

Odysseus and a band of warriors then concealed themselves inside the horse, which was offered as a gift to the Trojans, who wheeled it into their city. When night fell, Odysseus and his men stole out of the horse and threw open Troy's city gates to the Achaian forces, who proceeded to sack the city of Troy and win the war.

The Trojan princess Kassandra, who could see the future, warned that the Achaian wooden horse was a trick; but because she had rejected the advances of the god Apollo, she was fated never to be believed.

ADOPTED GODS

Aeneas, son of the goddess Venus, fled Troy and settled near the River Tiber in Italy. During a visit to the underworld, he was shown a parade of the souls of the great Romans-to-be.

The ancient Romans, conscious that their own civilization was of relatively recent origin, set great store by foundation myths that connected Rome to the great cultures of the past. The first great ancestor of all things Roman, they believed, was Aeneas, a Trojan prince, who escaped from the sack of Troy (see pages 42–43). The Romans tended to overlook the elements of their culture that derived from the Etruscans, and instead emphasized their links with Troy and Greece.

LINE OF DESCENT

The Romans adopted the Greek mythology and the Greek gods wholesale, which is why most of the classical gods have two names, one Greek, one Roman. Zeus (see pages 30–31, 34–35) became Jupiter, Hera changed to Juno, Poseidon (see pages 33, 34) became Neptune, Athena (see pages 36–37) became Minerva, and so on. Not all these identifications are exact, for the Roman gods and goddesses have their own histories and natures. The chief triad of Jupiter, Juno and Minerva, worshipped on the Capitoline hill, was probably of Etruscan origin.

The Romans traced a line of descent from Aeneas through the legendary kings of Alba Longa to the twins Romulus and Remus. The new-born twins were thrown into the River Tiber by their uncle, Amulius, who wanted to be the next ruler.

Romulus and Remus were rescued from the River Tiber by a she-wolf, who suckled them. Later, they were found by a shepherd, Faustulus. When the boys were old enough, Faustulus told them their history. The twins then killed Amulius.

A SIGN FROM THE GODS

Romulus and Remus did not drown, and when they were older they killed their uncle. They then decided to build a new city by the River Tiber. Romulus climbed the Palatine hill, and Remus the Aventine hill, and they waited for a sign from the gods. Remus saw six vultures, but Romulus saw 12. Romulus claimed that the gods favoured him, and began to plough a furrow to mark the city's limits. When Remus jeered at him, and jumped over the furrow, Romulus killed him.

STEALING SABINES

When Romulus' idea of opening Rome as a sanctuary for refugees and outlaws attracted many men but no women, he was faced with a problem. He solved it by instituting a new festival, the Consualia, in honour of the Roman harvest god Consus. He invited a neighbouring tribe, the Sabines, to attend. While the Sabine men were absorbed in the chariot races, at a pre-arranged signal the Romans seized the Sabine women and carried them struggling across the thresholds of their houses.

The Sabine men, furious at this trick, laid siege to Rome under their king, Titus Tatius. Eventually they broke through the city's defences. The bloody battle that followed was only stopped by the Sabine women, who ran out between the two armies – their Sabine fathers and their new Roman husbands – and begged them to stop. So the two sides made peace, and the next king after Romulus was a Sabine, Numa Pompilius*.

* (see page 48)

The traditional date for the foundation of Rome (Colosseum, left) is 753BCE. Romulus declared his city a sanctuary, and soon built up a population of outlaws. The only problem was the lack of women, and this was solved by stealing wives (right) from the nearby Sabine tribe. Once the city was established, the god Mars took Romulus away in his chariot, to become a god.

THE SACRED FIRE

The most essential elements of Roman religion focussed on the home and the homestead, with the paterfamilias, the head of the family, in the priestly role. The home was sacred to the Romans, and the heart of the home was the hearth. It was the wife's role each evening to clean the hearth, and bury the burning embers under ashes so that the fire would last until morning.

Every element of a Roman house had its own god. Cardea, for instance, was the goddess of the door hinges. All these household gods were presided over by the spirit of the head of the household. Each household also had its Lares (shrine to Lares, left) and Penates, protective spirits which probably originated in early ancestor worship.

THE VESTAL VIRGINS

Vesta was the goddess of the hearth, the Roman equivalent of Greek Hestia. Because the Romans revered the household, Vesta was immensely important in Roman religion, and her priestesses, the Vestal Virgins, were regarded with the greatest respect. They were so sacred that if they walked past a condemned man, he was pardoned.

There were six Vestal Virgins, girls from respected families who were chosen by the High Priest to serve the goddess for 30 years. They played an important part in many festivals, but their chief role was to maintain the sacred fire in Vesta's hearth. This fire was thought to symbolize Rome's eternal power. If the fire went out, the Vestals had to rekindle it by rubbing two sticks together. This way of making fire was a link to the past, as was the round shape of Vesta's temple, which recalled the round huts of Rome's earliest settlement.

The Penates, the gods of the storecupboard, were twin protective spirits of the household. A portion of every meal was offered to them on the flames of the hearth. The Roman state also had its own Penates, the Penates Publici. They were the protectors of Rome, and according to myth had been rescued from the flames of Troy by Aeneas (below).

THE SOUL OF ROME

As the name suggests, the Vestal Virgins could not marry, and one who broke her vows was punished by being buried alive. According to mythology, a number of Vestals were wrongly accused, but saved themselves by calling on the goddess to help them.

The Vestals represented the very soul of Rome. But Emperor Gratian (ruled from CE367 to 378), who was hostile to the pagan religions, ceased to pay the Vestals their salaries, diverting the money instead to the imperial postal service. Worship of the pagan gods was officially banned by Emperor Theodosius (ruled from CE379 to 395) in CE394, and the fire of Vesta went out for good.

The temple of Vesta (ruin, left) was a small circular building in the Forum, the centre of Roman life. Its shape and design reminded Romans of Rome's earliest buildings, huts with wooden posts and thatched roofs. The Vestal Virgins lived next door, in a large building arranged around one central courtyard.

CLAUDIA'S PRAYER

One of the greatest foreign deities introduced to Rome was Cybele*, the great mother. Detailed preparations were made to welcome the boat carrying the statue of the goddess. The whole city, including the Vestal Virgins, went down to the mouth of the River Tiber to meet the boat. But when it arrived, the boat grounded in the muddy shallows of the river. Men tugged and strained at the tow rope, but the boat was stuck fast.

One of the Vestal Virgins, named Claudia Quinta, about whom there was a lot of wicked gossip, stepped forward and, scooping water from the river, poured it over her head three times. She prayed to her goddess, Vesta, 'Mother of the gods, they say I am not chaste. If I am guilty, condemn me, and I will pay for it with my life. But if I am innocent, demonstrate it now!' Claudia removed the sash from around her waist and tied it to the tow rope. As soon as she gave a slight tug on the rope, the boat lifted from the river bed, and allowed her to pull the statue into the city.

* Cybele's (see pages 50–51) cult statue was brought to Rome from Phrygia in 204BCE.

Numa's Religion

Although imperial Rome seems to us a city ahead of its time, the ancient Romans themselves stressed their agricultural heritage. It was the dream of many Romans to retire from city life to their farm in the countryside. Many Roman poems celebrate country life, and the mythology of agriculture is very rich. The old agricultural religion of the Latin tribes was called 'the religion of Numa', after King Numa who succeeded Romulus, Rome's founder (see pages 44–45). Numa Pompilius (715–672BCE) was the founder of Roman religion.

Ceres (above) was often jointly worshipped with Tellus, also called Terra Mater, mother earth. She was said to have discovered grain and to have given it to Triptolemos to distribute to humankind – a story similar to the Greek myth of Demeter (see pages 38–39). In fact, during a famine in 496BCE, a prophecy identified Ceres with the Greek goddess Demeter.

Gods of the countryside

Before sowing, Roman farmers offered a cup of wine and a joint of roast meat to Jupiter (see page 44). Before harvest, they sacrificed a sow to the corn goddess Ceres, and made offerings to Jupiter and Juno.

Jupiter and Tellus were 'the great parents without whom nothing would grow'. Bacchus ripened the grapes. Robigus and Flora kept the blight from the trees and enabled them to fruit. Minerva protected the olive trees. Venus was the goddess of the garden, while Lympha, the goddess of fountains, provided irrigation. And Bonus Eventus, the god of good fortune, provided good luck, without which no amount of hard work would come to anything.

Flora (left) was the goddess of flowers and the spring. According to the poet Ovid (c.43BCE), she was originally a nymph named Chloris. Zephyrus, the west wind, fell in love with her, and his gentle kiss transformed her into Flora. When she breathed out, she spread flowers all over the earth. While Flora was the goddess of the blossom, Pomona was the goddess of the fruit. She was the wife of Vertumnus, an Etruscan god of the changing seasons, regarded by the Romans as the god of orchards.

Faunus and Silvanus were both gods of the woods, hunting and agriculture. Silvanus, who is usually shown with three nymphs known as the Silvanae, became a god of the fields when his woodland was cleared and cultivated. Faunus (above, right), the god of the forests, remained a wilder, more dangerous figure; he was also a god of prophecy and fertility.

GODS OF WILD THINGS

There was also a host of lesser agricultural gods. When ploughing, for instance, the Romans prayed to Vervactor when turning over fallow land. But of all these deities, the most important was the corn goddess Ceres.

Besides the gods of agriculture, the Romans worshipped the gods of wild things. Faunus, the Latin god of the forest and of flocks, became identified with the Greek god Pan. Those who slept in Faunus' sacred groves might have the future revealed to them in dreams. There was also a goddess, Fauna, who was thought to be either the wife, sister or daughter of Faunus. Fauna came to be identified with the earth and the fertility goddess Bona Dea, the good goddess, who was worshipped exclusively by women.

POMONA'S HEART

Pomona was a wood nymph who loved her apple orchard. She always had a knife in her hand, which she used to prune a branch or take a cutting. Wishing to be left alone, she built a fence around the orchard, so that no one would enter.

The god Vertumnus walked past one day and was dazzled by her beauty. He fell in love with her at that moment. From then on, every day he passed by her fence in a different disguise. One day he was a harvester, with a basket overflowing with corn. The next he was a haymaker, with a wisp of hay behind his ear. But Pomona never even gave him a second glance.

Finally, Vertumnus turned himself into an old woman and dared to enter Pomona's orchard. Sitting down with her beneath an apple tree, he urged Pomona to take the hand of the god Vertumnus, for he was the first to grow the apples that she loved, and therefore was the only one who would truly understand her.

Vertumnus' words melted Pomona's heart, and when he turned himself back into his true form – a young man as radiant as the sun – she agreed to marry him.

Gods from Abroad

Having merged the Latin and Etruscan gods with those of Greece, the Romans proved more than willing to incorporate gods from other cultures with which they came into contact. Egyptian, Phrygian, Arab and Celtic gods mingled with the classical Roman deities. Some, such as Arsu, the Arab war god, had a limited following. Others, such as Cybele, the Phrygian mother goddess, were worshipped across the empire. For a few years, Elagabal, the Syrian sun god, was the most important god in Rome.

The Romans worshipped the Egyptian goddess Isis as the single manifestation of all gods and goddesses. She was worshipped in association with her husband Serapis, who was the Egyptian god Osiris (see pages 144–145).

The Phrygian Goddess

Cybele was called the Magna Mater, the great mother, and, like the Egyptian goddess Isis (see pages 144–145), she was the mother of the gods. Cybele was originally the great goddess of Phrygia, now Anatolia in Turkey. Her cult was brought to Rome (see page 47) in 204BCE because an oracle prophesied that the invading Carthaginian troops, under Hannibal (247–183BCE), would be driven from Italy if Cybele was embraced by Rome.

Despite the defeat of the Carthaginians, many Romans were suspicious of this foreign goddess. Until the reign of Emperor Claudius (CE41–54), Romans were forbidden to serve as Cybele's priests. But her cult, with its ecstatic dances, spread right across the Roman empire.

The main focus of Cybele's mythology was the death and resurrection of her companion Attis. This myth related to the Mesopotamian myth of Inanna and Dumuzi (see pages 68–69). Cybele was a goddess of fertility and nature, and the mistress of all wild things. In Roman times, she was shown with a pair of lions; often the lions are drawing her carriage.

Roman soldiers were fanatically devoted to the god Mithras (above), the ruler of the cosmos, whose ultimate origins were in ancient Persia. Mithraism was a mystery religion, with seven grades of initiation, but many of its secrets are now lost. The central myth involved Mithras slaying a bull, from which new life sprang.

The Roman emperor Claudius (coin, right) was particularly interested in Phrygian religion, and encouraged the worship of Cybele (below). In contrast, his successor, Emperor Nero (ruled from CE54 to 68), preferred the similar Syrian goddess Atagartis.

THE SYRIAN GOD

It was a Syrian god who threatened to usurp all the other gods of Rome. This was Elagabal, the invincible sun. Elagabal had been worshipped at Emesa, now Hims in the Syrian desert. Elagabal's time came when Septimius Severus became emperor of Rome (ruled CE193–211). Septimius, who had served in the Syrian army, and paid his respects at the shrine of Elagabal, was married to Julia Domna (CE170–217), the daughter of Elagabal's high priest.

Julia Domna's son, Emperor Caracalla, was assassinated in CE217. But her sister, Julia Maesa, managed to have her grandson, Bassianus, declared emperor. However, Bassianus (CE204–222) had inherited Elagabal's priesthood and would not leave the service of his god. So the black stone of Elagabal, which was actually a black meteorite, was removed from the shrine at Emesa and taken to Rome.

The attempt of Bassianus to establish Elagabal as the supreme god of Rome did not last long. His grandmother, worried about his psychopathic behaviour, had him murdered in CE222. Then the new emperor, Severus Alexander (ruled from CE222–235), sent the stone of Elagabal back to Emesa.

Bassianus decreed that the name of Elagabal, the invincible sun (right), was to be invoked before that of any other god. The Romans nicknamed their new emperor Heliogabalus, the scoundrel of the sun.

51

THE CELTIC CHIEF

The Celts were widely distributed across Europe from the beginning of the Iron Age, around 1000BCE. They were a warlike people, distinguished from their Slavic, Germanic and Italic neighbours by a culture of heroism and hospitality that is clearly depicted in their surviving mythology. Moving westwards from their homeland in central Europe, the Celts soon dominated much of non-Mediterranean Europe, particularly France, where they were known to the Romans as the Gauls. By the 3rd century BCE, the Celts held sway from Galicia in Asia Minor in the east, to Ireland in the west.

Epona (left) was the Celtic horse goddess. She was worshipped all over the Romano-Celtic world, and even had her own festival in Rome. Always shown with at least one horse, she was associated with fertility and with the dead.

THE IRISH MYTHS

After the defeat of the Celtic leader Vercingetorix (d.46BCE) by the Roman emperor Julius Caesar (100–44BCE) in 52BCE, the spirit of the Celtic tribes was crushed, and they were gradually pushed to the western and northern margins of their territories: Brittany in France; Wales, Cornwall and Scotland in the United Kingdom; and Galicia in Spain. Only in the isolation of Ireland did the culture of the Iron Age Celts survive into the age of written records.

By the time the Irish myths were first written down in the 8th century CE, Irish society had been transformed by the arrival of Christianity in the 5th century CE, and Viking raiders from Scandinavia in the years that followed. Luckily, the Irish tradition of storytelling meant that the myths were handed down relatively intact.

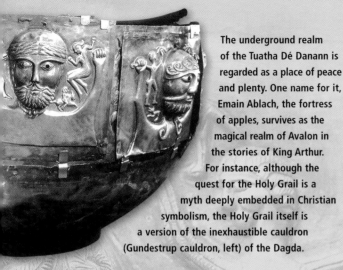

The underground realm of the Tuatha Dé Danann is regarded as a place of peace and plenty. One name for it, Emain Ablach, the fortress of apples, survives as the magical realm of Avalon in the stories of King Arthur. For instance, although the quest for the Holy Grail is a myth deeply embedded in Christian symbolism, the Holy Grail itself is a version of the inexhaustible cauldron (Gundestrup cauldron, left) of the Dagda.

THE GOOD GOD

By contrast, we know very little about the myths or the druidic religion of the Celts in France or Britain. One of the few deities who appears on numerous inscriptions from the Celtic world is Sucellus, whose name means the 'good striker'. He carries a hammer and a pot, or cauldron.

The Irish equivalent of Sucellus is the Dagda, the good god. Like Sucellus, he oversaw the weather and the harvest. Instead of a hammer, he carried a huge club. One end of the Dagda's club killed the living; the other end revived the dead. He also had a great cauldron that provided an inexhaustible supply of food for his followers.

In the Irish myths, the Dagda is the chief of the Tuatha Dé Danann, the people of the goddess Danu. They are said to be a race of divine beings, who inhabited Ireland before the Celts.

After the coming of the Tuatha Dé Danann retreated to the otherworld, where they became transformed in folk tales into the fairies. According to myth, Brug na Bóinne (left), Newgrange at County Meath, is one of the burial chambers that acts as a gateway to the magical otherworld of the Tuatha Dé Danann.

THE KINGSHIP

The Dagda, the king of the Tuatha Dé Danann, fell in love with Bóand, but she was married to Elcmar, who lived at Brug na Bóinne. In order to have Bóand for himself, the Dagda sent Elcmar away on a quest, and laid a spell on him so that he would not notice the passing of time. Elcmar thought he was gone for only a single night, but he was actually away for nine months, and in that time the Dagda and Bóand had a baby son, Angus. When Angus was grown, the Dagda told him to go to Brug na Bóinne and claim his kingdom from Elcmar.

'Go ready to fight,' said the Dagda, 'but do not do so if Elcmar will agree to let you rule as king for a day and a night.'

This Angus did; and Elcmar agreed. But when Elcmar came after the day and night to reclaim his kingdom, Brug na Bóinne, Angus refused him. 'You gave me the kingship for a day and a night,' he said, 'and it is in days and nights that the world passes.'

So Angus retained the kingship of Brug na Bóinne forever, a day and a night at a time.

THE RISE OF THE VIKINGS

The Vikings thrived in Scandinavia from around CE800 to 1100. They were an extraordinary people, who combined farming and lawmaking with ferocious treasure-hunting raids and daring voyages of discovery. Their myths are still alive in everyday English, for the words Tuesday, Wednesday, Thursday and Friday recall some of the chief Viking gods: Tyr, the god of war; Odin, the father of the gods; Thor, the god of thunder; and Frigg, Odin's wife.

THE GIANT FROM ICE

Viking mythology tells of both the beginning of the world and of its coming destruction (see pages 60–61). Both events are described with imagery that vividly evokes the icy landscape of Scandinavia, with its mountains and glaciers.

At the beginning of time, the Vikings imagined two opposing realms, one of ice and one of fire. Between these domains was the Gap – a great nothingness. From the ice realm of Niflheim flowed rivers heavy with poison, which built up layer by layer in the Gap. And from the fire realm of Muspell came fiery sparks and dancing airflows.

Where the cold winds from the north met the hot winds from the south, they carved the poison ice into the shape of a man. This was Ymir, the father of the frost giants and the rock giants. Ymir slept and, as he slept, he sweated. From his sweat, a man and a woman grew under his left arm. They were the first giants, the enemies of the Viking gods.

The icy realm of Niflheim was said to have existed many ages before earth was created. In its midst was the spring Hvergelmir, from which the poison rivers flowed. It was from the ice of these rivers that the first giant, Ymir, was formed.

The creation of humanity

The frost giants lived where four rivers of milk joined together. The rivers flowed from the magical cow Audhumla, which lived in the ice realm of Niflheim. When Audhumla licked the ice into the shape of a man she created Buri, the first of the Viking gods. Bestla, one of the younger frost giants, fell in love with Buri and they had three sons, Odin*, Vili and Ve, who became Viking gods.

One day, Odin, Vili and Ve decided to kill Ymir, Bestla's frost giant father. So much blood flowed from Ymir's fatal wounds that it drowned all the frost giants, except one family who escaped in a boat. Odin and his brothers then created Middle Earth, the world of man, using Ymir's body to make the earth, his blood to create the sea, and his skull to make the sky. They also created the first man and woman from driftwood logs of ash and elm that they found lying on the beach.

* (see pages 58–59)

The last barbarians

The Viking gods have their origins in the Germanic gods of northern Europe. Woden, or Wotan, and Thunor, or Donar, were the chief gods of the Germanic peoples by the 1st century CE. But the Viking goddesses owed much to the Danish fertility goddess Nerthus.

The barbarian Germanic tribes, such as the Angles, the Saxons, the Franks, the Vandals and the Visigoths, exploited the decline and fall of the Roman empire from the 4th to the 6th century to establish their own kingdoms. As they transformed from tribal warrior-bands into great nations – such as that of Anglo-Saxon England – they also gave up their old tribal beliefs in favour of Christianity. Therefore, by the 8th century, the heathen religion of Woden had been supplanted in Europe by the new faith.

In the far north, however, the old religion still held sway, and the rise of the Vikings in Scandinavia may be seen as the last glorious gasp of the old Germanic spirit.

The Viking myths did not represent a religion with a set theology. Instead, individual humans could ally themselves with the various gods to gain inspiration, strength and good fortune. Sacrifices to the gods were a way of obtaining their favour, in battle, love or life. The gods could be honoured in temples or out of doors, in forests, on hills or mountains, or by springs.

THE VANIR AND THE AESIR

The Vikings are often seen as violent and bloodthirsty because their seafaring raids brought such terror to their victims. Yet they were essentially a farming people. They had strong laws, which gave many rights to women, and established the first parliament at Thingvellir in Iceland. This majestic spot straddles the mid-Atlantic ridge, where the North American and European continental plates are shearing apart from each other.

The Althing – the Viking parliament – first met at Thingvellir (above) in CE930. It was an open-air meeting of all the free men, and met every two weeks over the summer to make laws and settle disputes.

The wolf Fenrir was bound with a magic chain by the gods, when it grew too strong for them to control. To gain Fenrir's trust, the god Tyr (right) put his right hand into the wolf's mouth, but it was bitten off. At the final battle of Ragnarok, Fenrir killed both Odin and Tyr, before swallowing the sun.

WAR AND PEACE

In Viking mythology, the gods are divided between those who are essentially gods of fertility and peace, and those who are basically gods of war. It is thought that the Vanir, the gods of fertility, were worshipped first, and that the rise of the war gods, the Aesir, came much later.

One myth tells of the war between the Vanir and the Aesir. It ended with a truce, but the clear winners were the Aesir, who were then joined by the chief Vanir gods. These were Njord, a god of the sea, and his son and daughter, Freyr and Freyja, the gods of peace, plenty and fertility.

Odin, the all-father, was the king of the Aesir. After he created humankind, Odin married Frigg, and their children were the Aesir, who included Thor, Tyr, Heimdall and Balder, the beautiful. Less is known about the Asyniur, the Aesir goddesses, though it is thought that they were just as revered.

THE TRICKSTER

There was one god, Loki, the shape-changing trickster, who belonged to neither the Aesir nor the Vanir. He was a joker whose pranks slowly turned sour. He engineered the death of Balder, and prevented him from being brought back to life. Hel, the underworld goddess, would not release Balder unless everyone wept for him; and Loki refused.

Loki's origins are unclear, but in the battle of Ragnarok (see pages 60–61) his allegiance lay with the giants. He had three children – the world serpent Jormungand, the blue-faced goddess of the underworld Hel, and the wolf Fenrir – by the giantess Angrboda.

The design of this smith's furnace stone, which protected the nozzle of the bellows from the heat of the furnace, shows Loki with his lips sewn shut by the dwarfs.

LOKI'S GIFTS

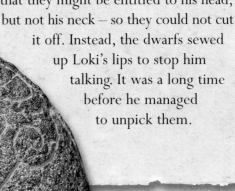

Thor adored his beautiful wife Sif, with her lovely mane of golden hair. But one day Loki, the trickster god, cut off Sif's hair. Thor was furious! To make amends, Loki promised to ask the dwarfs to forge her new hair. He went to the finest dwarf craftsmen, Brokk and Eitri, and asked them to make treasures for the gods.

Brokk made new hair for Sif and a spear that would hit any target. Eitri made a magical gold arm ring. He also created a hammer that would crush anything it struck, and never miss its target. The gods were delighted with the gifts. Odin kept the spear and the arm ring, and Thor the hammer and the new hair for Sif.

But when the dwarfs realized that they would not be paid, they demanded Loki's head. Loki argued that they might be entitled to his head, but not his neck – so they could not cut it off. Instead, the dwarfs sewed up Loki's lips to stop him talking. It was a long time before he managed to unpick them.

THE WORLD TREE

The Vikings believed that at the centre of the universe was a great tree, named Yggdrasil. This was the backbone of the world. Yggdrasil had three roots: one in Asgard, the home of the gods; one in Jotunheim, the home of the giants; and one in Niflheim, the realm of ice. According to Viking mythology, Asgard was linked to Middle Earth, the home of humankind, by Bifrost, the rainbow bridge.

ROOTS AND REALMS

Gnawing at the roots of Yggdrasil was an evil serpent, Nidhogg. At the top of the tree sat an eagle, Hraesvelg, surveying the whole of creation. The flapping of the eagle's wings caused the winds in the world of men.

Beneath each of the three tree roots lay a spring. Under the root in Niflheim was the poison spring that first filled the Gap, the nothingness between fire and ice at the beginning of the world (see pages 54–55). Under the root in Jotunheim was the well of wisdom. And under the root in Asgard was the well of fate, where the three Norns – Fate, Being and Necessity – lived. They shaped the lives of men and women from birth to death. They also watered the tree every day with pure water from the well of wisdom, thus keeping it alive. This water fell onto the earth as dew, to sustain and refresh the world.

The world tree, Yggdrasil (above), was a giant evergreen that linked the worlds of gods, giants and men. Ygg, the terrible, is another name for Odin. A giant evergreen tree stood outside the temple of Odin, Thor and Freyr in Uppsala, Sweden. Each Viking farm also had its own protective tree.

Days in Odin's great hall of Valhalla were spent fighting to the death, but each evening the warriors were restored to life. They could then spend the night feasting and drinking mead. The warriors of Valhalla were called the Einheriar. They only left Valhalla to fight in the mythical final battle of Ragnarok, when the warriors and the gods fought the powers of the underworld.

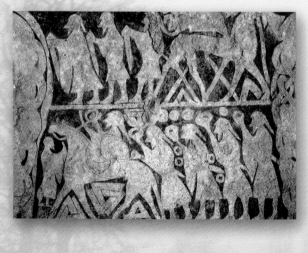

WORLDS APART

Yggdrasil supported the realms of gods, giants and the dead – just as the temples of the gods were supported by great tree-trunk pillars. The myths of the Vikings are largely set in these realms, rather than in Middle Earth where humankind lived.

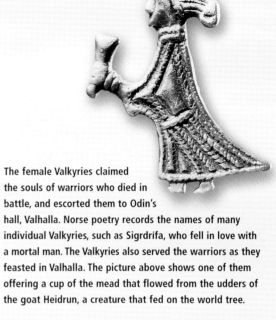

The female Valkyries claimed the souls of warriors who died in battle, and escorted them to Odin's hall, Valhalla. Norse poetry records the names of many individual Valkyries, such as Sigrdrífa, who fell in love with a mortal man. The Valkyries also served the warriors as they feasted in Valhalla. The picture above shows one of them offering a cup of the mead that flowed from the udders of the goat Heidrun, a creature that fed on the world tree.

DEATH AWAITS

Middle Earth was linked to Asgard by the rainbow bridge, and there were ways for human beings to get there. One way was to die in battle. Viking warriors – who were socially superior to the peasants – hoped to be selected by the Valkyries, female spirits whose name means 'choosers of the slain', to go to live in Odin's great hall of Valhalla. There, warriors were always ready for the final battle at the end of the world.

A second way to join the gods, and avoid the terrors of the underworld, was to die a sacrificial death. This was open to women as well as men.

Odin was the god of battles and the dead, but also of poetry, inspiration and magic. Sitting in his high seat, with his two ravens, Thought and Memory, whispering secrets in his ears, he thirsted for knowledge. He traded one of his eyes for a single mouthful from the spring of wisdom. He also hung for nine days and nine nights on the world tree, pierced through with a spear. At the height of his agony, he reached out and seized the runes that the Vikings used for both writing and divination. These runes gave him many powers.

TWILIGHT OF THE GODS

Pagan Vikings in the 10th century CE wore small hammer amulets around their necks, to secure the protection of Thor. These hammers were similar to the crucifixes worn by European Christians. In fact, silversmiths cast both hammers and crosses in the same moulds. In the transitional period between paganism and Christianity, many Norsemen hedged their bets. Records show that one Viking, Helgi the Skinny, said that he 'believed in Christ, but prayed to Thor on sea journeys, and in tough situations'.

This image of Christ on the cross (right) is on the reverse of a Viking amulet, showing a split allegiance between Christ and the pagan gods. In carvings and poems, the suffering of Odin on Yggdrasil (see pages 58–59) was equated to that of Christ on the cross. Loki was seen as the devil.

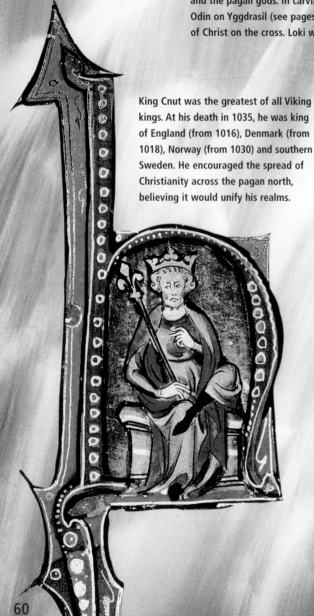

King Cnut was the greatest of all Viking kings. At his death in 1035, he was king of England (from 1016), Denmark (from 1018), Norway (from 1030) and southern Sweden. He encouraged the spread of Christianity across the pagan north, believing it would unify his realms.

THE GODS ARE DEFEATED

The Vikings turned to Christianity partly because it offered a surer promise for the afterlife, and partly for practical reasons of trade and politics. When King Cnut of Denmark conquered England in 1016, he was happy to convert in order to keep his new kingdom. Norway converted in the 10th and 11th centuries. The Althing in Iceland voted for Christianity in 1000. Uppsala in Sweden, where the great temple of Odin, Thor and Freyr once stood, was ruled by a Christian bishop by 1164.

This was a true twilight of the gods. By 1300, the Viking gods had been eclipsed by Christianity. Their worship survived only in scattered fragments of folk religion and superstition.

But the gods themselves were prepared for such a fate. Their own mythology anticipated the final battle of Ragnarok, in which they would fight with all their strength, but be defeated. It was also prophesied that Loki would lead the hordes from the underworld, in a ship made from dead people's nails, and that the wolf Fenrir would swallow the sun.

RAGNAROK

In the last battle, the war god Tyr was not able to fight because the wolf Fenrir had bitten off his right hand. Thor died while trying to kill the world serpent Jormungand. Loki and Heimdall killed each other, and Fenrir devoured Odin. Finally, Surt, who had waited at the fiery gates of Muspell since the dawn of time, set the world ablaze.

Then a new sun was born, and a new earth rose from the sea. To this young land came Odin's sons Vidar and Vali, and Thor's sons Modi and Magni, the only survivors of the last battle. They were joined by Balder, the beautiful, released from the underworld at last, with his blind brother Hoder by his side. Together, they stood where gold-roofed Asgard used to be. In the grass they found the golden chess pieces with which the Aesir used to play, and wept for the glory days.

The 12th-century Viking chessmen (left), found on the Isle of Lewis in the Outer Hebrides, were carved in Norway from walrus ivory. Among the masterpieces of Viking art, they recall the fabled golden chessmen of the gods. Chess replaced an earlier Viking board game called hnefatafl, in which a king with a small army had to defend himself against a large attacking force.

The myth of Ragnarok tells of the defeat of the gods. At the end, Yggdrasil, the world tree, shelters one man and one woman from the destruction. Their names are Lif and Lifthrasir, and from them a new race of humans are born.

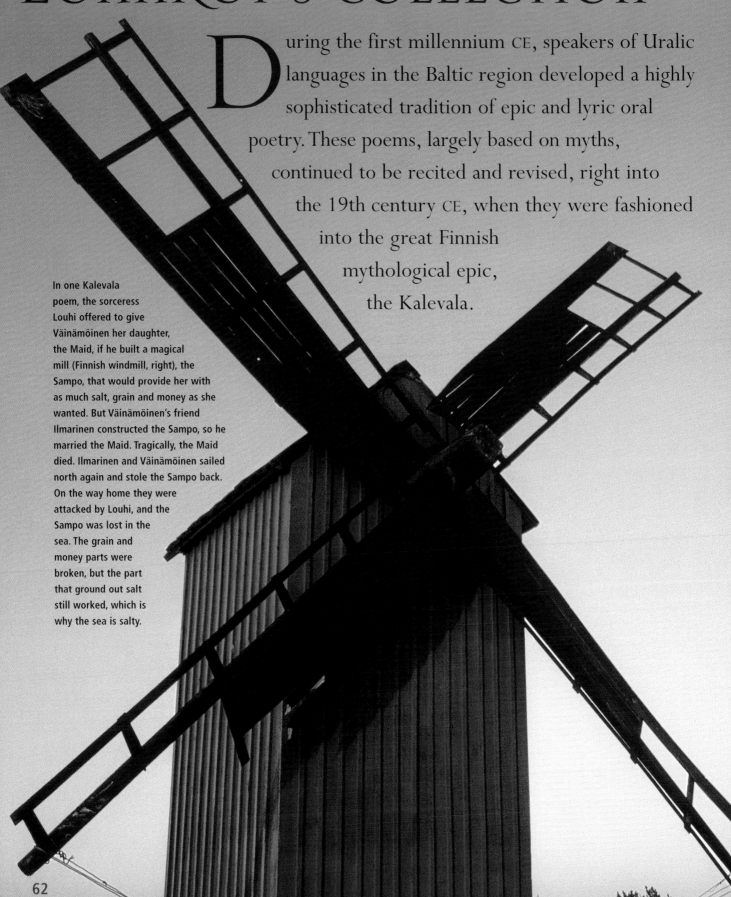

Lönnrot's collection

During the first millennium CE, speakers of Uralic languages in the Baltic region developed a highly sophisticated tradition of epic and lyric oral poetry. These poems, largely based on myths, continued to be recited and revised, right into the 19th century CE, when they were fashioned into the great Finnish mythological epic, the Kalevala.

In one Kalevala poem, the sorceress Louhi offered to give Väinämöinen her daughter, the Maid, if he built a magical mill (Finnish windmill, right), the Sampo, that would provide her with as much salt, grain and money as she wanted. But Väinämöinen's friend Ilmarinen constructed the Sampo, so he married the Maid. Tragically, the Maid died. Ilmarinen and Väinämöinen sailed north again and stole the Sampo back. On the way home they were attacked by Louhi, and the Sampo was lost in the sea. The grain and money parts were broken, but the part that ground out salt still worked, which is why the sea is salty.

WEEPING PEARLS

Väinämöinen was sailing to the Northland with Ilmarinen and Lemminkäinen when his boat became stuck on an object in the sea. Looking down, they saw that it was lodged on the shoulders of a giant pike. Lemminkäinen drew his sword, swung it back, and dealt the fish a mighty blow. But his sword just rebounded, he toppled over into the sea, and Väinämöinen had to pull him out like a drowned rat. Väinämöinen then drew his own sword and cut the pike in two. They cooked and ate the flesh, and Väinämöinen used the pike's jawbone and teeth to make a kantele* that nobody else could play but him. When Väinämöinen played, the animals danced, and Tapio, the lord of the forest, climbed to the top of a mountain to listen. Väinämöinen himself was so moved by his own playing that he wept tears that turned into pearls.

* A kantele is a zither-like instrument that is still played throughout the east Baltic nations, and was used to accompany the Kalevala poetry.

NATIONAL IDENTITY

These poems were written down from the lips of illiterate peasants, largely in Karelia, in eastern Finland and the Russian northwestern borderlands, and Ingria, in Russia, south of the Gulf of Finland. That they survived at all is due largely to the tolerance of the Orthodox church, whose priests in these eastern regions allowed a poetry that Catholics and Lutherans further west tried to stamp out as pagan.

The poems of the Kalevala (first published in 1835) were collected by Elias Lönnrot (1802–1884) as a statement and celebration of national identity, and the book still retains this status today. Finland had been a province of Sweden since the 12th century CE, annexed by Russia in 1819, then a Grand Duchy of the

Väinämöinen (right) was a great singer, but one day a younger rival, Joukahainen, challenged him to a singing match. Angered, Väinämöinen sang the young man into a swamp, and would not release him until Joukahainen offered him his sister Aino's hand in marriage. But Aino was horrified at the idea of marrying such an old man, and she drowned herself in the sea.

Russian Czar, and by 1917 an independent republic. Before Lönnrot published the Kalevala, most Finns had probably never heard of the mythological heroes such as Väinämöinen, the first man, who was already old by the time he was born. He was a great singer, and spent much of his time singing songs of creation – singing the world into being.

Perun's thunder

The Slavic nations of eastern Europe are diverse peoples all sharing a common ethnic and linguistic origin, and whose folklore and mythology reflect a common religious heritage. They were first described as a separate people in the 2nd century CE. There are three branches of Slavic culture: eastern, including the Russians and Ukrainians; southern, for instance the Serbians and Slovenians; and western, such as the Slovakians, Poles and Czechs.

A residue of pagan belief still underlies Russian folk rituals and beliefs, and mingles with the teachings of the Orthodox church. For instance, Egorii, also known as Saint George, was not simply a dragon slayer in Russian folklore, but, as Springtime Egorii, he was a god-like figure who unlocked the earth after the frosts of winter.

Good and evil

One of the most interesting features of Slavic mythology is its dualism. The world is seen as ruled by opposing deities of good and evil. Slavic creation stories, even after 1,000 years of Christianity, often show God and the Devil creating the world together.

The chief god of the Slavic pagans was known in Russia as Perun, the lord of the universe. Often described as the thunder god, Perun has been compared to both the Norse Thor (see pages 54–61) and the Greek Zeus (see pages 34–35). He was believed to send thunder and lightning, and also the rain that makes the crops grow. His sacred tree was the oak, perhaps because oaks are often struck by lightning.

The god Perun, too important to eastern Slavic culture to be utterly forgotten, lived on in folk belief as the prophet Ilya (fiery ascension of Ilya, left), also known as Elijah, who sent the thunder and lightning. In one widespread rain-making ritual, which survived the official worship of Perun, a maiden dressed only in flowers whirled in the middle of a ring of people, beseeching the god, as the prophet Ilya, to send rain.

The turning point for eastern Slavic paganism came in CE988, when Prince Vladimir of Kiev (CE956–1015) was baptised as a Christian. Most Slavic easterners, and many southerners, now belong to the Russian Orthodox church; in the west, people are mainly Roman Catholics. The conversion of the people to Christianity occurred gradually between the 8th and 13th centuries CE. Where pagan beliefs proved impossible to stamp out, they were incorporated in folk religion.

THE LAUME'S WHIP

Once there was a young carpenter who roamed the world in the company of Perkun* and the Devil. Perkun thundered and flashed lightning to keep the wild beasts away, the Devil hunted for food, and the carpenter cooked it. After a while they found a good place to settle down, so they built a hut and planted turnips.

But after a few days they realized that someone was stealing their turnips. Both the Devil and Perkun kept watch, but the thief thrashed them with a whip. Then the carpenter tried. He took his fiddle with him, and passed the time by playing tunes. The thief, who was a laume, a sort of supernatural hag, appeared to him and asked him for a music lesson. 'You can't play the fiddle with gnarled old fingers,' said the carpenter. 'Put them in that split tree-stump, and I'll straighten them out.' When the hag put her fingers in the split tree-stump, the carpenter knocked out the wedge of wood, that was keeping the split open, and trapped her fingers. Once she had promised never to return and bother them, he let her go. But he kept her whip.

The carpenter, Perkun and the Devil decided to separate, but they could not agree who should keep the hut. They decided it should go to the one who was the most frightening. First the Devil raised such an unearthly commotion that it frightened Perkun into fits; but the carpenter bravely held out. Then Perkun threw lightning that made the Devil hide under the bed; but the carpenter strongly held out. Eventually it was the carpenter's turn. He cracked the hag's whip, and imitated her voice. Perkun and the Devil ran, leaving the carpenter with the hut.

*This story comes from Lithuania, where Perun was called Perkun.

ARCTIC OCEAN

RUSSIAN FEDERATION

EUROPE

A dragon

Shen Nong

CHINA

HIMALAYAS

Marduk

Gilgamesh

Brahma

İRAQ

Inanna

Shiva

Khupning-Knam

Spirit gates

Nanga Baiga

İNDİA

GOLDEN TRIANGLE

AFRICA

Rama

MALAYSIA

Tohan

İNDİAN OCEAN

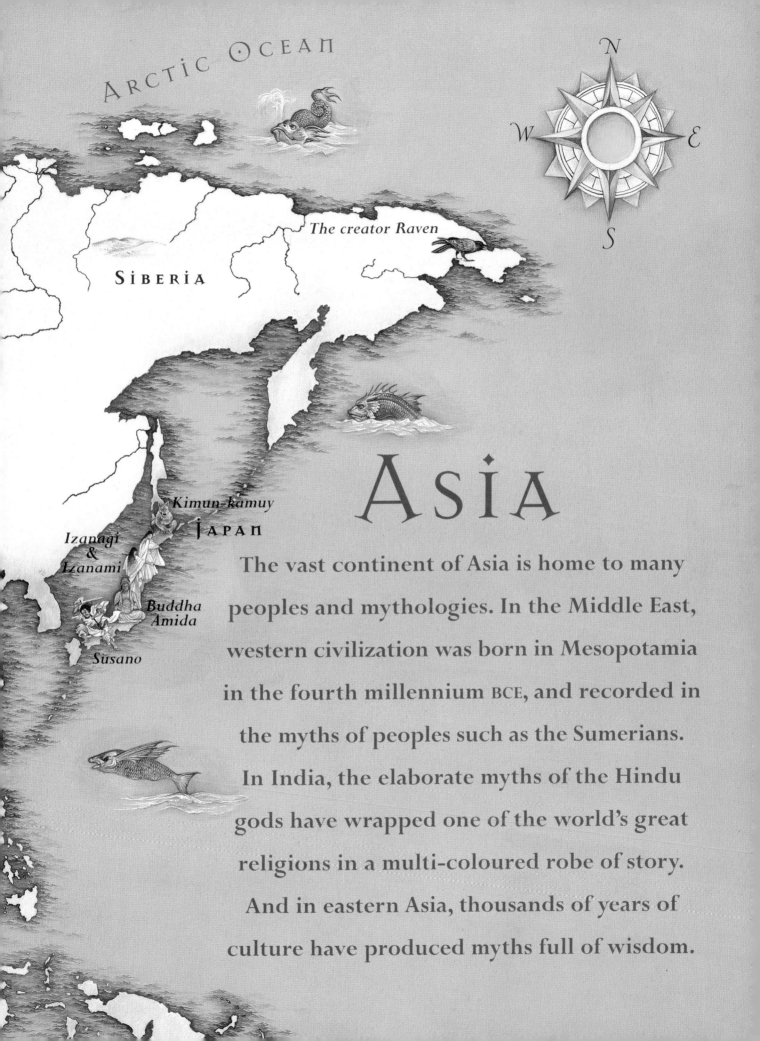

ARCTIC OCEAN

N

W E

S

SIBERIA

The creator Raven

Kimun-kamuy

JAPAN

Izanagi & Izanami

Buddha Amida

Susano

ASIA

The vast continent of Asia is home to many
peoples and mythologies. In the Middle East,
western civilization was born in Mesopotamia
in the fourth millennium BCE, and recorded in
the myths of peoples such as the Sumerians.
In India, the elaborate myths of the Hindu
gods have wrapped one of the world's great
religions in a multi-coloured robe of story.
And in eastern Asia, thousands of years of
culture have produced myths full of wisdom.

THE SHEPHERD'S WIFE

Ancient Mesopotamia – modern Iraq – was the cradle of western civilization. The Ubaidians first settled the fertile valleys between the rivers Tigris and Euphrates in the fifth millennium BCE. They were supplanted around 3300BCE by the Sumerian people, who established the first cities, such as Uruk, the city of the god-king Gilgamesh (see pages 72–73).

It was the dream of the Sumerians (worshipping Sumerian, below) to transform the dry land of Sumer into something resembling the paradise garden of Dilmun. They feared both flood and drought. Each year, the dry season threatened to turn their land into a parched desert, which is how the Sumerians imagined the underworld.

It was Enlil, the Sumerian high god, who persuaded the council of gods to create a new flood to drown humankind. But the water god Enki warned Ziusidra, the king of Sippar, to build a boat. Ziusidra, the sole survivor of the flood, was granted eternal life in Dilmun.

GODS AND KINGS

The city-state was at the root of Sumerian culture. Each city was protected by its own god, represented by the king, who was able through the priesthood to interact with the great gods on behalf of the people. The basic mythology of ancient Sumer was adapted in turn by the later Mesopotamian civilizations: the Akkadians, Babylonians, Assyrians, Canaanites and Hittites. The same gods and themes recur, though sometimes under different names.

Mesopotamian cultures flourished because they reclaimed fertile agricultural land, from flood plains between the rivers, by draining and irrigating. This act of turning water into land was a continuation of the process by which the Sumerians believed the earth itself had been created from the primal flood.

Inanna and Dumuzi

The key myth of Inanna, the goddess of fertility, and the shepherd Dumuzi provided the Sumerians with a mythological assurance that spring would come again. Each New Year, the king of Uruk and the high priestess of Inanna, the lady of heaven, re-enacted the marriage between the shepherd Dumuzi and the goddess. This was thought to ensure the fertility of the land for that year.

The annual death of Dumuzi was marked with mourning rites. The spectacle of women weeping for him is mentioned in the Bible in *Ezekiel 8:14*.

Like most of the Sumerian myths, that of Inanna and Dumuzi survived the extinction of Sumer itself. In 1750BCE, Hammurabi, king of Babylon, became the sole ruler of ancient Sumer. The Babylonians absorbed much of Sumerian culture, including the mythology. To them, Inanna and Dumuzi were known as Ishtar and Tammuz, but the story remained very much the same.

Every autumn, Dumuzi's descent to the underworld marked the arrival of the dry season in which nothing would grow. But although he died each year, in spring he emerged again, once more to marry the goddess of fertility, Inanna (above). This enabled the crops to grow.

THE DESCENT OF INANNA

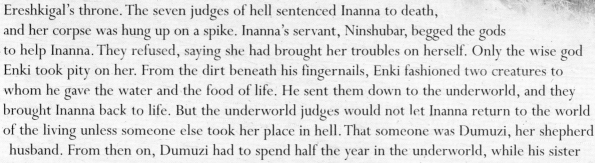

Although the goddess Inanna feared she would die if she entered the underworld, she descended into it to challenge the ruler, her sister Ereshkigal. At the seven doors of hell, Inanna was stripped of her clothes and jewels, and the seven Tablets of Destiny, which she was carrying, until she arrived naked and defenceless before Ereshkigal's throne. The seven judges of hell sentenced Inanna to death, and her corpse was hung up on a spike. Inanna's servant, Ninshubar, begged the gods to help Inanna. They refused, saying she had brought her troubles on herself. Only the wise god Enki took pity on her. From the dirt beneath his fingernails, Enki fashioned two creatures to whom he gave the water and the food of life. He sent them down to the underworld, and they brought Inanna back to life. But the underworld judges would not let Inanna return to the world of the living unless someone else took her place in hell. That someone was Dumuzi, her shepherd husband. From then on, Dumuzi had to spend half the year in the underworld, while his sister Geshtinanna took his place for the other half; she became the scribe of the underworld.

Marduk's triumph

The kingdom of Babylonia thrived in southern Mesopotamia from around 2200 to 538BCE, when the Persians conquered the city. The Babylonians, inheritors of the great cultural legacy of ancient Sumer (see pages 68–69), were a supremely confident people. The great creation epic of Babylon, which was chanted before the statue of Marduk, Babylon's chief god, celebrated the foundation of the world, and of Babylon itself, which was the centre of the world.

The Babylonians believed that Marduk attacked Tiamat and cut her in two halves, from which he formed the sky and the earth. The rivers Tigris and Euphrates (above) sprang from her eyes. The other gods then accepted Marduk as their king.

The city of Babylon

Little now remains of the once-great city of Babylon; just a cluster of mud banks by the River Euphrates, south of modern Baghdad, Iraq. But in its heyday the city of Babylon was a breathtaking sight. Its famous 'hanging gardens' were one of the wonders of the ancient world, and the ancient Greek historian Herodotus (c.480–425BCE) wrote that such was its magnificence that no other city could match it.

At the heart of the city was the temple of Marduk, the House of the Foundation of Heaven and Earth, which sat near the ziggurat, the tower, within the Esagila, the temple complex.

So intimately were the city and the god entwined that the first action of any conquering army was to carry off the statue of Marduk, thus plunging the city into mourning.

When King Sennacherib of Assyria (ruled from 704 to 681BCE) conquered the city in 691BCE, the myths of Marduk were reattributed to the Assyrian god Assur.

The great new year festival of Babylon, held at the time of the spring equinox, celebrated the victory of Marduk (far left) over the dragon Tiamat (left), and allowed Marduk once more to fulfil his role in ordering the universe, by settling the destinies of the stars and planets for another year.

THE DEATH OF TIAMAT

The rituals enacted by the people of Babylon recreated
Marduk's battle against the creator Tiamat. According
to a Babylonian myth, there were two seas, the sweet
water and the salt, which were named Apsu and Tiamat.
They created, amongst many other things, Anu, the god
of the heavens, and Ea, the god of earth and water.

But Apsu and Tiamat were disturbed by the noise of the
younger gods. Apsu tried to destroy them, but instead Ea slew
Apsu. Tiamat was enraged by the killing of her husband, and
raised an army of monsters, including a dragon (a form of
Tiamat herself), against Ea and his son Marduk. Leading Tiamat's
army was the god Kingu, carrying the Tablets of Destiny.

After a long fight, Marduk managed to kill both Tiamat
and Kingu. He seized the Tablets of Destiny and created
humankind from Kingu's blood, mixed with earth.

The Babylonians believed
that once Marduk had used
the power of the Tablets
of Destiny to establish the
cosmos, he founded the city
of Babylon to be his home.

THE KING OF URUK

A pair of bull-men hold up a winged solar disc, probably representing the sun god Shamash. In the myth of Gilgamesh, Shamash helps Gilgamesh and Enkidu slay the demon Humbaba. In the centre is the figure of the hairy hero Lahmu, who was associated with Ea, the god of wisdom. Enkidu's name means 'created by Ea', and this, as well as his hairiness, connects him with Lahmu.

For the Babylonians, as for the Sumerians before them, the king held his authority directly from the gods. For instance, King Hammurabi (see page 69) claimed to have received the laws enshrined in the *Code of Hammurabi* directly from the hand of the sun god Shamash. Kings were so important that, in recent years, the dictator Saddam Hussein (b.1937) partly justified his rule of modern Iraq by comparing himself to King Nebuchadnezzar, who ruled from 605 to 562BCE.

Gilgamesh's city of Uruk lies 250km southeast of modern Baghdad. Excavations suggest that the city was founded around 3500BCE. It was in cities such as Uruk that humankind first developed the kind of urban civilization that we live in today. At the heart of Uruk was the temple of the goddess Ishtar (see pages 68–69), the House of Heaven.

GILGAMESH'S QUEST

The king whose name meant most to successive Mesopotamian civilizations was Gilgamesh, the mythical king of Uruk, now called Warka. He was said to be two-thirds a god and one-third a man. Uruk was the city of the sky god Anu and Ishtar, the goddess of love (see pages 68–69). Gilgamesh's own mother was said to have been a goddess, but his father was a man. From his mother, he inherited his divine powers; from his father, his mortality.

The first stories about him were written down by 2150BCE, and eventually they were all joined together in what is now known as the epic of Gilgamesh. This long and exciting story exists in various forms in the Sumerian, Akkadian, Babylonian, Elamite, Hittite and Hurrian languages. The overriding theme is one of intense interest to every human being: the inevitability of death.

Gilgamesh, who feared death after his best friend died, set out on a quest for the secret of eternal life. He eventually discovered a plant that would make an old man young again. On the way home, Gilgamesh bathed in a pool, and a snake stole the plant and ate it. According to this ancient Mesopotamian myth, that was why snakes could shed their skins and become young again; but men aged and died.

Gilgamesh and Enkidu

The people of Uruk were constantly complaining to the gods about Gilgamesh, their arrogant king. In order to appease them, Aruru, the goddess of creation, fashioned from clay a man, Enkidu, to be Gilgamesh's rival. Enkidu lived like a wild beast in the hills, until a priestess of Ishtar tamed him. Then she took him to Uruk to challenge Gilgamesh. After a long fight, Gilgamesh won. But the gods could not have predicted what happened next – they became friends.

Gilgamesh and Enkidu had many adventures, such as slaying the demon Humbaba, a ferocious creature with a face of coiled intestines and breath like fire. It was after this event that Ishtar, the goddess of love, fell in love with Gilgamesh, but he spurned her advances. Furious, she went to Anu, her father, and begged him to send down the Bull of Heaven to destroy Gilgamesh.

But Enkidu and Gilgamesh managed to defeat the magical bull. They then cut out the bull's heart and offered it to the sun god Shamash. The gods decreed that they must pay for this sacrilege: Enkidu fell sick and died; Gilgamesh was thrown into misery by Enkidu's death, and set out in vain to discover the secret of eternal life.

THE SUPREME BEING

The mythology of the Hindu gods is one of the richest in the world. The complex nature of the great gods such as Brahma, the creator, Vishnu, the preserver, and Shiva, the destroyer, is played out in myths full of action, adventure and romance. These myths embody the subtle and generous spirit of Hinduism itself.

According to myth, at the very centre of the world is Mount Meru (above), at whose summit is the heaven of the god Brahma. Meru is encircled by the River Ganges.

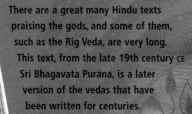

There are a great many Hindu texts praising the gods, and some of them, such as the Rig Veda, are very long. This text, from the late 19th century CE Sri Bhagavata Puràna, is a later version of the vedas that have been written for centuries.

Hinduism

India is a large country with a vast population of over one billion people, speaking 745 different languages. About 80 per cent of this population is Hindu. Hinduism as a religion seems to have its early roots in the Indus civilization (c.2500–1500BCE), which already worshipped Shiva, the god of creation and destruction, and Devi, the great goddess. These early gods were then fused with the Vedic gods of the Aryans, who invaded India around 1700BCE.

The first Hindu myths were written down in religious texts such as the Rig Veda around 1200BCE, and the stories continued to be developed for 2,000 years. They are still an element of Hindu belief today.

All the other Hindu gods are part of Brahma (centre). In fact, the great gods Vishnu (reclining on the snake Ananta with his wife Lakshmi) and Shiva, although they have very different characters and roles in the myths, cannot truly be distinguished from Brahma himself. Therefore, Shiva may be worshipped as Mahadeva, the great god, and Vishnu as Prajapati, the lord of creation.

BRAHMA'S CREATION

Brahma is the supreme being of Hinduism, and the source of all space-time, which works in never-ending cycles. When Brahma wakes and breathes out, the visible world comes into being, for a day which lasts over four billion years; when he falls asleep, the world dissolves back to nothingness, waiting to be created again when Brahma wakes once more.

The physical world, our world, which Brahma breathes out, is an illusion, for everything in it is still part of Brahma.

* Brahma (above)
** Ganges
(see pages 76–77)

THE FIRST MAN

Manu, the first man created by Brahma*, became a great sage after 10,000 years of meditation. Brahma was so impressed he told Manu to wish for whatever he wanted. Manu asked, 'When the world comes to an end, let me protect all the beings in it.'

One day, when Manu dipped his hands into his washing water, he caught a fish, which begged him to save it. He put the fish into a jar, but it grew too large, so he put it into the River Ganges**. But the fish outgrew the river, so Manu took it to the ocean, where the fish revealed that it was Brahma himself. It warned Manu that the world would soon be flooded, and told him to build an ark, and to place in it the seeds of life. The ark came to a halt on the summit of the highest peak of the Himalayas, and when the flood receded, Manu began the work of creating the world anew.

SACRED SITES

India is full of sacred sites called tirthas, which means 'places where one fords a river'. Hindus believe rivers carry sacred power through the land, and the greatest of all these rivers is the Ganges (see page 75), which rises in the Himalayas and winds across northern India to spill into the Bay of Bengal. There are many holy sites along the Ganges' 2,507km length, of which the greatest is Varanasi, the city of Shiva, where the faithful go to bathe in the river.

Hindus say that bathing in the Ganges (above) is like being in heaven. As a consequence, many pilgrims gather to bathe in the waters, which are likened to amrita, the elixir of life.

The 60,000 sons of King Sagara (right) were sent to search for their father's missing horse. They dug down to the world beneath Patala, the earth, and found the horse there, together with the sage Kapila. When the sons accused him of theft, Kapila burned them to ash with the rays from his eyes.

Shiva (below, left) lives on Mount Kailasa with his wife, the goddess Parvati (below, right), the gentle daughter of the mountain. His two children are Skanda, also known as Kartikeya, the god of war, and elephant-headed Ganesh, the remover of obstacles. Ganesh is one of the most popular of the Hindu gods, and people often pray to him at the start of any new enterprise, hoping he will put their case to Shiva, his father.

FROM HEAVEN TO EARTH

The Ganges and her sister rivers carry water down from the Himalayas to irrigate the crops and keep India's population fed. As far back as the Rig Veda (see page 74), it was said that India's rivers originated in heaven. The Hindus believe the River Ganges is the earthly manifestation of the goddess Ganga.

One myth tells how Ganga came down to earth from heaven. A certain King Sagara had 60,000 sons, who were burned to ash by the sage Kapila. Sagara's great-great-great-grandson, Bhagiratha, himself became a sage, and so impressed Ganga that she appeared to him in human form, and agreed to descend and purify the ashes of Sagara's 60,000 sons. However, she was so mighty that if she fell directly to earth she would destroy it.

THE ELEPHANT-HEADED GOD

The goddess Parvati, the wife of Shiva, wanted to ensure that she would have complete privacy whilst having her bath. So she rubbed dirt and oil from her body, fashioned it into a plump little being, and sprinkled over it holy water from the River Ganges to bring it to life. Thus, she created her son Ganesh. Parvati ordered him to stop anyone from entering her bathroom.

When Parvati's husband Shiva arrived, Ganesh dutifully blocked his way. Angered, Shiva opened the third eye on his forehead, which blazes with the fire of ten million suns, and burned off Ganesh's head. When he realised what he had done, Shiva gave Ganesh* an elephant's head.

* Ganesh used one of his own tusks to
  write the holy book the Mahabharata.

Ganesh (below) never exerts himself more than necessary. Once, he had a bet with his brother Skanda over who could travel around the world and find out the most about the wonders of the world. The winner would win Siddhi (success) and Buddhi (intelligence) as his brides. Skanda set off on the long journey, but Ganesh stayed at home and read. When Skanda returned, Ganesh was waiting to tell him all the wonders of the world that he had read about, and so won the bet.

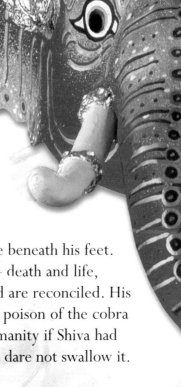

The god Shiva was persuaded to allow Ganga, in her earthly form as a river, to pass through his hair, dividing into many streams as she fell to earth.

As Mahakala, the lord of time, Shiva is responsible for both the creation and destruction of all things. He is often depicted dancing in a circle of fire, trampling the dwarf of human ignorance beneath his feet.

Shiva is a god in whom all opposites – death and life, good and evil, light and dark – meet and are reconciled. His throat is blue, for he holds in it the blue poison of the cobra Vasuki, which would have destroyed humanity if Shiva had not taken it into his mouth – but even he dare not swallow it.

THE LIFE OF RAMA

The greatest hero of Hindu mythology is Prince Rama. The story of his quest for his wife Sita, who was abducted by the demon Ravana, is told all over India. It was first written down in the 50,000-line Sanskrit epic the Ramayana (200BCE—CE200). In the 16th century CE, the story was re-told in Hindi by the poet Tulsi Das (1541–1605), and this version is still recited by professional storytellers today.

Rama, Sita and Lakshmana are shown here with Hanuman, the monkey general whose courage helped Rama win Sita back.

In Thailand, they have their own version of the Ramayana called the Ramakien, composed in the late 1700s by King Rama I (1782–1809). The Ramakien has become the national epic of Thailand. This version has a happy ending, for Nang Seeda (Sita) reappears from under the earth once more to be the wife of Phra Ram (Rama, pictured below fighting Ravana's demon army).

RAMA AND VISHNU

Rama and his three brothers, Bharata, Lakshmana and Shatrughna, were born to King Dasharatha of Ayodya and his three wives, after Brahma asked the god Vishnu to vanquish the demon king Ravana. Rama himself has one half of Vishnu's divinity, and his brothers share the rest. Hindus worship Rama as a god in his own right, an incarnation of the god Vishnu.

The brothers grew up unaware of their divine origin. Rama fell in love with Sita, the daughter of King Janaka of Mithila. She is an incarnation of Vishnu's faithful wife Lakshmi.

THE ARMY OF RAKSHASHAS

Because of an incident at court, Rama, Lakshmana and Sita went to live quietly in the forest. All was well until the demon king Ravana kidnapped Sita, who called out to the trees of the forest to tell Rama that she was being taken against her will. She also threw her jewels and her gold veil to five monkeys, and it was with the help of Sugriva, the monkey king, and Hanuman, his general, that Rama won Sita back.

Rama besieged Lanka, Ravana's city, with an army of monkeys led by Hanuman, who had already set fire to the city, having found Sita and given her Rama's ring as a token. Ravana's army of demonic rakshashas, was full of ferocious warriors with names like Death-to-Men. They were all vanquished in a fierce battle. Rama then shot Ravana with a magic arrow.

Rama could not overcome the demon king himself. The sage Agastya advised him to worship the sun, the source of all life. He did this, and also borrowed the chariot and charioteer of the sky god Indra. Then Rama went after Ravana (above, with Rama and Sita) relentlessly. Eventually, Rama shot the demon king with a magic arrow forged by Brahma.

SITA IN EXILE

When Rama defeated Ravana, Brahma appeared and told Rama that he was really Vishnu, and that Sita was actually Lakshmi. But although the stage was set for a happy ending, it was not to be. Rama and Sita returned to Ayodya and ruled there for 10,000 years until, one day, he discovered people were still gossiping about Sita and Ravana. Angered, Rama banished Sita. In exile, she gave birth to his twin sons. Years later, Rama saw his sons and he asked Sita to return. But her heart was broken, and she sank into the earth. Rama ruled for another 1,000 years before returning to the gods.

The story of Rama has spread far beyond India. It is popular in Indonesia and Malaysia, though most of the people are Muslims, and in Thailand, though most of the Thais are Buddhists.

Forest guardians

The indigenous tribal peoples of India are collectively known as the Adivasis. One of these tribes is the Baiga, who live in the forests of the Mandla hills in southeastern Madhya Pradesh, central India. They are a gentle and peaceful people, numbering approximately 10,000. The myths of the Baiga are the foundation of Baiga life and thought, and are the reason they have maintained their cultural identity to the present day.

The creator Bhagavan told the Baigas that they would never be rich, for if they did they would forsake the earth. Today, the Baigas are still desperately poor, but as one destitute Baiga put it, 'The whole world belongs to us; we are the real masters, for the Baiga is Bhumia Raja, the lord of the earth'.

Creating the world

The Baiga believe that they have lived as guardians of the forest since the dawn of time, and call themselves the sons and daughters of Dharti Mata, mother earth. The founder and culture hero of the Baiga, called Nanga Baiga, was, they say, the very first man on earth. He was born in the forest from Dharti Mata herself, and nursed beneath a clump of bamboos by Bamboo Girl, who gave him a golden axe to play with. Nanga Baigin, the first woman, was born alongside him.

Nanga Baiga and Nanga Baigin played a crucial role in the formation of the world. Bhagavan, the creator, had spread the world out flat like a chapati, a type of flat bread, but it flapped about everywhere and would not stay still. But Nanga Baiga and Nanga Baigin took four great nails and drove them into the four corners of the earth to steady it.

Nanga Baiga (left, possibly shown with Nanga Baigin) helped to create humankind, and to teach them how to live. He was the first magician. Today, the Baigas are regarded as gunia, magicians, who can keep a tiger (main image) out of a village.

THE BAIGA BELIEFS

Because they trace their ancestry directly to Dharti Mata, the Baiga thought it was wrong to tear her body, the earth, with a plough. Instead, they hunted in the forest, and practised a form of slash-and-burn agriculture known as bewar. The Baiga would cut down an area of forest, set fire to the wood when it was dry, and then sow their seeds in the ashes. Every three years, they moved to another patch of forest. The area of the bewar was always sacred.

From the middle of the 19th century CE, the Baiga came into conflict with forest officials, who restricted bewar agriculture to the 10,000 hectare reservation of Baiga Chak in the uplands of the Mandla hills, where many Baiga now live. At the same time, their forest rights were severely restricted. When the government took the forest from them, the Baiga said the Kali Yug, the age of darkness, had begun.

THE FOREST LORDS

In the days before there was any fire in the world, when the Baiga still ate their food raw, there was a ghost who had a sick child. The ghost went to a Baiga village to visit the medicine man, who looked in his winnowing-fan, saw the cause of the ghost-child's sickness, and cured him. The ghost then asked him what reward he would like. The man said, 'We eat our food raw, and it twists our bellies.'

The ghost gave him two small clay pots and an iron bangle and said, 'Make a pile of wood, and place the bangle in the middle of it and the pots on top, and your problem will be solved.'

The man gathered wood, and placed the bangle in amongst the wood. Fire came from the bangle, and he cooked a hot meal. Since then, no Baiga eats their food raw.

THE FIRST HOUSE

The Singpho people number about 15,000 in Assam and Arunachal Pradesh, in the foothills of the Himalayas in northeastern India. They are linguistically and culturally part of the Kachin people, who live in greater numbers in Myanmar and southwestern China. The Singpho are Buddhists, though they have also retained earlier shamanistic beliefs, making sacrifices of animals, such as bulls and pigs, to appease the Nats, their spirits.

FESTIVAL OF SONG AND DANCE

Although proud to be Indians, the Singpho also fear the loss of their cultural identity, surrounded as they are by much larger populations of Hindus, Muslims and Christians. Each year, about 2,000 Singpho gather together to celebrate their ancestors and their culture in the Shapawng Yawng Manar Poi festival. They dance the Thongka Manou, the Singpho folk dance, and feast on buffalo meat and rice under a huge awning of bamboo poles and palm leaves.

At festivals throughout the year, the Singpho make sacrifices to the spirits. They also celebrate the Buddhist New Year festival of Songken each April.

The Singpho live in houses built of wood and bamboo and thatched with leaves, just like the first ever house described in the myth opposite.

TRIBAL MYTHS

The Singpho retain many of their tribal myths, including a vivid account of the creation of the world. This tells of a time when there was no earth or sky, just cloud and mist. From this, a cloud-woman named Khupning-Knam was born. She in turn gave birth to two snow-children, a girl named Ningon-Chinun and a boy named Tung-Kam-Waisun.

New skills

When the Singpho left the heavenly plateau they were homeless. Two men, named Kindru-Lalim and Kincha-Lali-Dam, decided to build houses. The men asked the animals for advice.

The elephant said, 'Cut wooden pillars as thick as my legs.'

The snake suggested, 'Cut bamboo poles as long and thin as me.'

The buffalo cow, standing by the bones of her dead husband, advised, 'Set cross-poles across the top to make a roof like the bones of this skeleton.'

Then a fish told them how to finish the house, 'Fetch leaves and put them on the roof, overlapping like my scales.'

Kindru-Lalim and Kincha-Lali-Dam went home and successfully built the first house.

The Moklum people who live near the Singpho, along the border with Myanmar, tell how the sky god Rang, the father of the sun and moon, originally made an elephant with wings. Whenever it flew down to earth, it broke the trees and crushed the crops. So Rang took the elephant's wings away and gave it legs made from plantain roots, and a pestle for a trunk.

The myths of the Singpho are distinguished by their poetic beauty, with many images drawn from the wild and mountainous landscape of the Himalayas. They tell of a time when there was no earth or sky, just cloud and mist.

Bamboo and wood

After the world was created, the supreme being Phan-Ningsang and the sky god Mathum-Matta explored it. Finding a gourd in the shape of a man, they broke it open, and many little people spilled out of it. These were the first humans, who lived with the gods on a high plateau, until there were too many of them. Then Mathum-Matta made them ladders of bamboo and wood, gold, silver or cane so that they could descend to the plains. Wealthier peoples, such as the Assamese, came down the ladders of silver and gold. But the Singphos descended using the strong ladder of bamboo and wood, and still make their houses from these materials today.

LIFE IN THE HILLS

The Golden Triangle is a forested mountainous area straddling the borders of Thailand, Laos and Myanmar. Notorious for its opium fields, it is home to a number of hilltribes, each with its own culture and mythology. Among the major tribes are the Hmong (Meo/Miao), Akha and Karen. Many of these peoples are thought to have originated in southwestern China, and drifted south.

When an Akha village changes site, after the ground has been exhausted in the previous location, the village priest must ask the spirits for permission to settle. The priest drops a raw egg to the ground. If it breaks, the Lord of Land and Water is content for the village to be built. If the egg fails to break, it means the Lord of Land and Water withholds permission.

All the hilltribes are facing real pressure to change. Economic development of the Golden Triangle region, tourism, evangelical missions and a potential AIDS epidemic all threaten their cultural identity. Their traditional slash-and-burn agriculture, which causes serious damage to the forest, is now discouraged, as is opium production, so the tribes are now being drawn into the market economy and the tourist trade. The hilltribes brought the practice of opium cultivation (from opium poppies) with them from China. Since 1959, when it was outlawed, opium production has been cut by more than 80 per cent, and replaced by food crops.

The problems that the tourist trade causes are shown by the way that the Padaung tribe, also known as the Kayan, have revived their tradition of artificially elongating the necks of their girls (right) and women with a series of brass rings. This deformation would have died out if tourists were not willing to pay to take photographs of the 'long-neck women'.

Tribal traditions

Like the other tribes, the Akha people try to maintain their traditional way of life. There are some 38,000 Akha in northern Thailand, 15,000 in Laos, 200,000 in Myanmar, and 250,000 in the Yunnan Province in southwest China. There are also one million Hani people in China, who are closely related to the Akha.

All the hilltribes, while influenced by religions such as Buddhism, believe in spirits who may be helpful or harmful. The village priest of an Akha village, the father of the village, draws his authority from his direct link to the creator Apoe Miyeh, the male ancestor. The priest is responsible for the welfare of the village, conducts its religious ceremonies, and maintains the sacred sites, such as the spirit gates which keep evil spirits out of the village. These gates, which are renewed every year, mark the boundary between the human and spirit worlds. They are sacred and must not be touched.

THE BOOK OF LIFE

Apoe Miyeh created the earth and the sky, and from the sky came a series of spirits, the last of whom, Sm-mi-o, created human beings. At first the humans knew nothing, but Apoe Miyeh handed out books to all the different peoples of the earth, containing everything they needed to know. The book given to the Akha was written on the skin of a water buffalo. But a time came when the Akha were so hungry, they decided to cook the buffalo skin and eat it. Now they do not rely on writing or books, for they carry the creator's wisdom in their stomachs.

85

TOHAN'S PEOPLE

The indigenous peoples of the tropical rainforest of peninsular Malaysia are collectively known as the Orang Asli. They comprise 18 separate ethnic groups, with their own languages and cultures, and together number about 105,000. One of these groups of hunter-gatherers, whose territory is now the Krau Game Reserve, central Pehang, is known as the Chewong.

Traditional Chewong houses are lean-to constructions made of bamboo and roofed with attap leaves. One myth tells of a witch-like bas called Ya'Popag who lived alone in her house in a rice field. She enticed a family one by one into her home and then ate them. She was burned to death by Bongso, the youngest child, who was one of her intended victims.

EARTH SEVEN

The Chewong call this world Earth Seven, and tell of other worlds both above and below. Simply by living on it, people make Earth Seven dirty, so every now and then Tohan, the superhuman being who created humankind, turns it upside down. He warns the people of the forest, and they turn into blossoms and fly up to Earth Six; everybody left on the ground drowns, and Tohan creates new people and a new earth.

HOW BAS WERE MADE

Tohan asked his servant Nabi to fashion the first people out of the earth. Then Tohan gave him the breath to make them live. Nabi carried the breath in his hand. Wanting to look at it, he opened his fist, and the breath escaped. So the two figures Nabi had made became bas. Nabi made two more figures, and this time carried Tohan's breath to them safely, so they became true humans. The bas are large and hairy, and have eyes in the back of their heads. They want to eat humans' ruwai, which means 'soul' or 'life force'.

Today, there are around 300 Chewong, who still hunt and gather on their traditional forest lands, though they also farm crops such as tapioca, sweet potatoes, papayas and red peppers.

THE CHEWONG TODAY

As with the other Orang Asli – which means 'original people' in Malay – the Chewong are under the control of the Malay government, through the Department of Orang Asli Affairs. The Orang Asli cannot even appoint their own headmen without government approval. The Orang Asli are under pressure to assimilate to the mainstream of Malay society by converting to Islam, and also fear the dispossession of their traditional lands. In response to these pressures, the gentle Orang Asli have joined together in the 15,000-strong Peninsular Malaysia Orang Asli Association, to stand up for their rights and help preserve their unique culture and mythology.

The first human beings were taught how to live by the biasal, the original people, superhuman beings who have always existed. It was one of them, the culture hero Yinlugen Bud, who gave the Chewong their most important rule, that food must always be shared. To eat alone is regarded as dangerous and wrong.

PEOPLE LIKE US

The Chewong view their gods and spirits as 'people like us', and they believe it is by collaboration between the people and the gods that the world is sustained and constantly renewed. The Chewong are a non-violent, non-competitive people, who have no words for war, fight, quarrel, crime or punishment.

However, there are dangerous spirits known as bas which plague humankind. The bas were made by mistake, when Tohan first tried to make human beings. Superhuman beings such as Tohan are said to have cool eyes, which can see the different worlds; Chewong shamans also have cool eyes, and so can see many things cloaked from the hot eyes of ordinary humans.

THE KAMI

The country of Japan is a chain of mountainous volcanic islands. The indigenous inhabitants are the Ainu (see pages 94–95), but the Japanese, who probably emigrated from Korea, supplanted them. According to legend, the first Japanese emperor, Jimmu, took power in 660BCE. From then, the culture and mythology, expressed through the Shinto religion, began to flourish.

Japan is comprised of four large islands – Hokkaido, Honshu, Kyushu and Shikoko – and a number of smaller ones. The goddess Izanami is said to have given birth to them, and also to the kami – gods, or sacred powers of nature – that rule them.

THE EARLIEST BOOK

Shinto was the official religion of Japan until 1945, and Shinto beliefs remain central to Japanese life. A follower of the religion regards the duty of daily life as matsuri, which means 'service to the kami', the gods.

The most important of the kami are Izanagi and Izanami, who are still regarded as the founders of Japan. Their story is told in the earliest Japanese book, the *Kojiki*, the record of ancient things, which was completed in CE712. The *Kojiki* explains that when heaven and earth were first divided, the first kami were born.

The wind god Fujin is shown with a bag containing the winds of the world slung across his shoulder. Fujin blew away the mists to reveal the new world created by Izanami and Izanagi.

The kami are worshipped in Shinto temples, which are remarkable for their simplicity. Each Shinto temple has a gateless entrance called a torii (above); this usually consists of a pair of upright posts and a crossbar.

THE BIRTH OF THE GODS

In the beginning, according to myth, Japan was an unformed oily mass that floated like a jellyfish. From this primeval ooze, reeds grew, and turned into the first kami. After seven generations of kami, Izanagi and Izanami, the Noble Male and the Noble Female, were born.

Izanagi and Izanami were given the task of solidifying the land. Standing on the Floating Bridge of Heaven, they created the mythical first island of Onogoro. They descended to this island and married. Izanami then gave birth to the various islands of Japan. After the islands had been born, she gave birth to more of the kami who would rule the islands – the gods of the seas and rivers, the winds, the trees, the mountains and the plains. It was the wind god Fujin who completed the creation of Japan, by blowing away the mist and revealing the islands.

In giving birth to Kagutsuchi, the god of fire, Izanami burned herself so badly that she died. Izanagi was furious, and cut off the head of the fire god with his sword. The fire god then erupted into 16 more gods, including those of rock, fire, thunder and water.

IZANAGI IN YOMI

When Izanami died, Izanagi followed her to Yomi, the land of gloom, and begged her to come back. Izanami said she would consult with the gods of Yomi, but asked Izanagi not to follow her. Izanagi ignored her request and broke off a tooth from a haircomb, to use as a torch to light his way. But when he found his wife, he saw that her body was full of squirming maggots. As the torchlight fell on them, the maggots became eight thunder gods. Horrified, Izanagi fled, with Izanami and her thunder gods in pursuit. When he reached the entrance to Yomi, Izanagi closed it with a huge boulder. From the other side, Izanami vowed to kill 1,000 people every day in vengeance; Izanagi, in turn, promised to create 1,500 new babies every day.

THE FIRST ANCESTOR

When Izanagi, the creator god, cleansed himself of filth from Yomi, the land of gloom (see pages 88–89), he created many new gods. When he washed his left eye, he created the sun goddess Amaterasu. When he washed his right eye, he created the moon god Tsuki-yomi. And when he washed his nose, he created Susano, the storm god. But Susano would not stop weeping for poor Izanami, and, in a rage, Izanagi banished him from heaven. Susano, in turn, committed acts of wanton destruction, such as desecrating his sister Amaterasu's weaving hall.

Prayers are left at the shrine of Amaterasu at Ise (above) to seek the favour of the goddess.

Hirohito (1901–1989) was the 124th emperor of Japan in direct lineage. After America occupied Japan at the end of WWII, Hirohito renounced his divinity, and the role of emperor became that of a constitutional monarch.

A DRUNK DRAGON

Susano is an ambiguous figure in Japanese mythology. Sometimes he is violent and destructive. At other times, he is a benevolent figure. When Susano descended to earth, his first act was to save the Rice Paddy Princess, Kusa-nada-hime, from the eight-headed dragon. He got the dragon drunk on sake, and cut it to pieces with his sword. When Susano cut off the dragon's tail, he found the sword Kusa-nagi, the grass-cutter, which he presented to his sister Amaterasu. This sword was one of the three great treasures of the Japanese imperial regalia, and is now kept at the Atsuta shrine, near Nagoya.

When Susano met a couple who told him that a dragon was about to devour their last daughter, Kusa-nada-hime, he turned their daughter into a comb, tucked her into his hair, slew the dragon, turned Kusa-nada-hime back into a girl, and married her.

Imperial treasures

Amaterasu is regarded as the first ancestor of the imperial family; the first emperor, Jimmu-tenno, was her great-great-great-grandson. This divine descent of the imperial family – which was publicly rejected by the late emperor Hirohito, after the 1945 defeat of the Japanese in WWII – was the founding stone of Japanese society. The emperor was regarded as the Son of Heaven, and ruled by divine right. Shinto became the state religion, and reverence for the emperor became a religious duty.

The chief shrine of Amaterasu for the last two millennia has been at Ise, in Mie Prefecture, where she was worshipped in early times as the Great Heaven Shining Deity. The shrine, which is considered to be the home of the goddess, is a simple, thatched, unpainted structure built of cypress. Every 20 years the shrine is completely rebuilt in exactly the same style, at an adjacent site, in an elaborate ceremony of renewal, the shikinen sengu. Originally worship at the shrine was restricted to members of the imperial family, but now it is a popular place of pilgrimage.

The shrine of Amaterasu at Ise (above) houses the mirror that dazzled Amaterasu with her own reflection when the gods lured her from her cave. This ancient mirror is regarded as the goddess herself. Amaterasu is regarded as the protective deity of Japan, the land of the rising sun. It is said that every Japanese person should visit the shrine at Ise at least once in their lifetime.

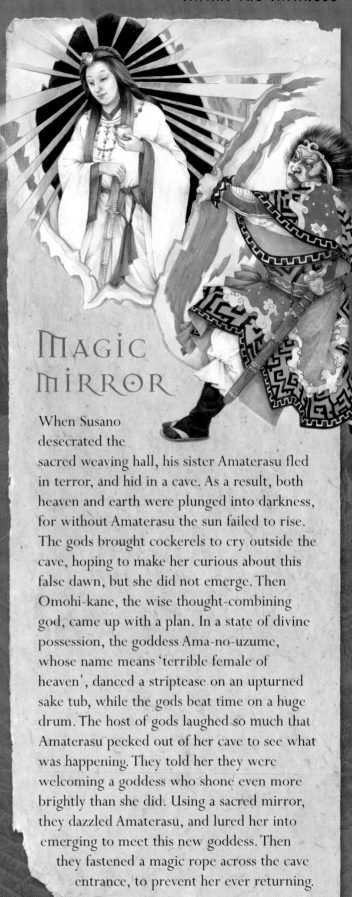

Magic mirror

When Susano desecrated the sacred weaving hall, his sister Amaterasu fled in terror, and hid in a cave. As a result, both heaven and earth were plunged into darkness, for without Amaterasu the sun failed to rise. The gods brought cockerels to cry outside the cave, hoping to make her curious about this false dawn, but she did not emerge. Then Omohi-kane, the wise thought-combining god, came up with a plan. In a state of divine possession, the goddess Ama-no-uzume, whose name means 'terrible female of heaven', danced a striptease on an upturned sake tub, while the gods beat time on a huge drum. The host of gods laughed so much that Amaterasu peeked out of her cave to see what was happening. They told her they were welcoming a goddess who shone even more brightly than she did. Using a sacred mirror, they dazzled Amaterasu, and lured her into emerging to meet this new goddess. Then they fastened a magic rope across the cave entrance, to prevent her ever returning.

Sacred slopes

The mountains are the most striking geographical feature of Japan, and have been regarded as sacred throughout Japanese history. According to Japanese mythology, the mountain god Oyamatsumi was born when the creator god Izanagi slew the fire god Kagutsuchi (see page 89). There are also gods of the high slopes, the low slopes, the steep slopes and the mountain base. Individual mountains have their own deities. Mount Miwa is the home of Okuninushi, the great land master, son-in-law of Susano (see pages 90–91). The most sacred mountain of all, Mount Fuji, is the home of the goddess Sengen-Sama.

Nitta Tadatsune explored one of the caves under Mount Fuji, and had a vision of Kannon, the goddess of mercy. But Sengen-Sama ordered him to leave her mountain home, or die.

The myth of Mount Fuji

Each July, around 1,000 worshippers still climb Mount Fuji to greet the dawn and pay homage to Sengen-Sama. The Japanese believe that she must be approached with reverence; one legend tells how the goddess slew the followers of the 12th-century CE hero Nitta Tadatsune when they trespassed on her territory. Tadatsune, warned by the goddess to retreat or meet the same fate, withdrew.

Mount Fuji is a dormant volcano, and one Shinto myth explains its origin. Long ago, an old man found a baby girl on the slopes of Mount Fuji, and named her Kaguya-Hime. She grew up to be so beautiful that she married the emperor. But after seven years she told him she was immortal, and must return to heaven. To console him, she gave him a mirror in which he would always be able to see her. Distraught, he tried to join her in heaven. Using the mirror, he followed her to the top of Mount Fuji, but he could go no further. His thwarted passion set the mirror ablaze, and since then smoke has always risen from the top of the mountain. Mount Fuji's last major eruption was in 1707.

The god of rice is called Inari, who can be depicted as a bearded man, as a woman or as a fox (right). Some households in districts along the coast of the Sea of Japan still keep foxes, which are regarded as Inari's messengers.

92

THE CONTEST

Mount Fuji and Mount Haku once fell out over which of them was taller. Mount Fuji said that she was; but Mount Haku insisted he was. The Buddha Amida was asked to give judgement. By running a water pipe from the peak of Mount Haku to the peak of Mount Fuji, he was able to show that Mount Haku was right, for water cascaded over Fuji. She was so angry at this indignity that she hit Mount Haku over the head, breaking him into eight peaks. That is why Mount Fuji is now the highest mountain in Japan.

A STAPLE FOOD

It is the plentiful supply of water from its mountains that maintains the still pools of water in Japan's paddy fields, which are necessary for rice to grow. Rice has always been Japan's staple food, and the best rice will only grow in mud submerged beneath water. The first rice seeds – together with silkworms, millet, red beans, wheat and soy beans – supposedly grew from the body of the food goddess Ogetsu.

The rice to be served at the coronation of the emperor was planted with special rites to call down the blessing of the gods on the crop and on his reign. Small Shinto shrines were built overlooking the rice fields, and all the implements used in preparing the fields, and in cultivating, harvesting and threshing the crop, were new.

Singing to the Gods

The Ainu (see pages 88–89) are the indigenous people of Japan. Today, 25,000 people identify themselves as Ainu in the Japanese census. Their hunter-gatherer way of life, with its deep respect for the spirits of the natural world, has affinities with that of the North Pacific cultures of the Inuit (see pages 104–105) and the Chukchi (see pages 100–101). Nowadays, the Ainu live largely on the northern Japanese island of Hokkaido.

Ainu men pray to the kamuy, often sprinkling a few drops of wine into the fire so that the fire goddess Fuchi will carry the prayer to one of the kamuy. Ainu women practise a form of shamanism in which the shaman (right) enters a trance and a god speaks through her mouth.

Every aspect of hunting, killing and eating an animal has a profound spiritual meaning for the Ainu. Bear cubs are ritually raised to be killed and eaten in the iyomante ceremony (left). After the ritual feast at which the bear is eaten, the god is sent back to his home with many gifts which will bring him wealth and status in the world of the gods. But to ensure that he will return, the final epic sung at the feast is cut short before the ending.

Adopting other cultures

Hokkaido belonged exclusively to the Ainu until 1868, the time of the Meiji Restoration, when Japan was modernized and opened up to foreigners. By 1899, the Ainu had lost most of their land and native rights. It was not until 1997 that new legislation, the Aino Shinpo, provided legal safeguards for the Ainu language and culture.

One of the key elements that has enabled the Ainu to survive in a hostile world is their ability to adopt elements from other cultures and 'make them Ainu'.

The Ainu have no tradition of writing, but instead a vast oral literature that has been passed from one generation to another. The epic songs known as kamuy yukar, songs of the gods, are mythological in nature, telling stories about gods and humankind.

A GOD'S VIEWPOINT

The Ainu gods are thought of as human in form, but in the myths they often take the guise of animals such as Kimun-kamuy, a bear, the master of the mountain. Almost uniquely in world literature, the Ainu kamuy yukar are sung in the first person, from the point of view of the god rather than of humankind.

To sing the songs of the gods is one way in which the Ainu can communicate with the kamuy, the non-human beings, with whom they share the physical world.

It is believed that while visiting the human world, the gods delight in watching humans dance (below) and listening to them sing the kamuy yukar. Though the richly meaningful iyomante bear ceremony is central to Ainu identity, and can be traced back hundreds of years, it was discontinued in most areas over the course of the 20th century CE.

BEAR'S SONG

I am Bear*, a mountain god. One day, my wife decided she wanted to visit the humans. I loved her so much, I followed her down in the shape of a bear, intending to destroy the human village. But from behind a tree in the village, an arrow flew, and struck my bear's body. I fell to the ground. When I came to, I was sitting in a tree, looking down at the body of a dead bear, the shape I had taken, lying on the ground below.

The human hunters prepared the body of the bear, and took it back to the village. I jumped down from the tree onto the back of one of the hunters, and he asked me to walk beside him. At a house in the centre of the village I was welcomed by Fuchi, the fire goddess, and invited in. The humans feasted, and gave me gifts. Eventually, they sent me home. I waited for two or three days, and my wife came after me, also loaded with gifts of wine and dumplings and ritual carvings. So we invited the other gods to a feast.

* Bear is known as Kimun-kamuy by the Ainu.

THE GIFT OF DISGUISE

At the centre of Ainu life were hunting rituals to appease gods such as Kimun-kamuy. When a god chooses to visit the land of humans, he does so disguised as an animal. Each god comes to trade with humankind. In return for gifts of wine and ritual artefacts carved from wood, the god leaves behind the gift of his animal form (the body). For example, Kimun-kamuy chooses the hunter who will kill him, and thus seals the bargain between god and man.

DRAGON TALES

Human beings have lived in China since around 3000BCE. It is now the most populous country on earth, with well over 1.3 billion citizens. Most of these are Han Chinese, but there are also over 50 minority peoples, each with their own beliefs and traditions. Since the foundation, in 1950, of the People's Republic of China by the communist leader Mao Zedong (1893–1976), China has been officially atheist, but religions such as Taoism and Buddhism are still widespread today.

Dragons were supposed to have particular power over water. The Chinese believed that they lived in lakes, rivers and the sea, but also in the sky, because they controlled the rain.

One myth claimed that dragons originated from carp that managed to swim up the Yellow river and leap the river heights at the Dragon Gate Mountain, a gorge that was hewn open by the hero Yu, mythical founder of the Xia dynasty that ruled China from around 2200 to 1700BCE. Yu was originally thought of as half-human, half-serpent, though later myths depict him as wholly human.

HALF-SERPENT

Many elements survive from the earliest Chinese mythologies. The Chinese still believe that dragons are benevolent creatures that bring good luck. Clay images of dragons or serpents – as Chinese dragons look like serpents – were worshipped in the 2nd century BCE; and Buddhism introduced the Dragon Kings of the Five Directions.

Many mythical figures were half-serpent, such as Nu Gua, the creator of humanity, whose myths were first recorded in the 4th century BCE.

Zhu Long, the Torch Dragon, was believed to have a human head but the body of a scarlet serpent. In the 4th century BCE, it was said that when he closed the vertical slits of his eyes the world grew dark; when he opened them, it grew light. Zhu Long neither ate, slept nor rested.

THE MYTHS TODAY

The classical myths of China – such as the creation of the earth from the body of the primal giant Pan Gu (see page 98) – were written down over 2,000 years ago. However, they have remained an active element in the way the Chinese think about and understand the world ever since. This is partly because the myths were understood as an essential part of history, but it is also because the three great religions of China – Confucianism, Taoism and Buddhism – mingled both with each other and with traditional folk religion to produce a rich soil in which myths could grow.

THE MANY MUD PEOPLE

In the beginning there were only two beings, Nu Gua and Fu Xi. They had the heads of human beings, but the bodies of serpents. They entwined themselves to become the first married couple. One day, Nu Gua scooped up some yellow clay and shaped it into the first human beings. She put the yellow clay creatures down, and they began to shout with joy. The next day she dragged a rope through the mud and splattered it about. This made many mud people*. The few people made from yellow clay were rich aristocrats, but the mud people were poor – and there were so many mud people.

When the fire god Zhu Rong and the water god Gong Gong had a battle, and destroyed the props that held up the heavens, Nu Gua could not bear to let the beings she had created die. She melted stones to fix the gaps in heaven, and killed a giant tortoise and used its four legs to prop up the sky again.

* Mud people from *Asian Field*,
March 2003, by Antony Gormley

THE GODS OF THE PEOPLE

For many thousands of years, China has depended on agriculture to keep its people fed. The earth, they believed, was made from the body of the primal giant Pan Gu, who was born from the cosmic egg of Yin and Yang, which is always shown as half-black (female) and half-white (male). The female and the male principles still form the basis of Confucianism, one of China's great religions (see page 97).

In the beginning, the whole universe was contained in an egg. From this was born the first being, the giant Pan Gu (see page 97). Pan Gu pushed the sky up from the earth, and then died from the exertion. His breath became the wind, his body the mountains, his blood the rivers, his hair the plants.

THE POISONING OF SHEN NONG

According to Chinese mythology, Shen Nong, the farmer god, taught humankind how to plough the land and plant grain. He was also the god of medicine, and personally tasted every single plant and every source of water, to find out which were beneficial and which were poisonous. Doing this, he poisoned himself 70 times in a single day. One herb was so toxic that even Shen Nong could not counteract it, and he died in the service of humankind.

Hou Ji, Lord Millet, was another god credited with teaching humankind the secrets of agriculture. He was also said to be the founder of the Zhou dynasty, which ruled China from 1050–221 BCE. He is praised for saving the Chinese people from starvation through his agricultural skill.

Shen Nong was the god of both agriculture and medicine. He founded Chinese medicine by testing every herb for poisonous or healing qualities. Because his body was transparent, he could see where each plant was having an effect.

In folk religion, aspects of the grain deity Hou Ji and the earth deity She, also known as Hou Tu, were fused in the worship of She Ji, the god of the ground and grain. Offerings (right) for a good harvest were made to She Ji by everyone, the emperor included. Every village had a shrine to the god – some simply a modest shrine with a bell and a tree, others an elaborate temple with dragons on the roof. Any family who had experienced some fortunate event, such as the birth of a baby, was expected to share their good luck with the god, making a gift of 'joyous gold' to fund a celebration in the temple. Such temples were for many hundreds of years the focal point of Chinese village life.

Hou Ji was born after his mother, Jiang Yuan, trod in the footprint of the great god Di. She brought him up to be a god of agriculture (agricultural scene, above).

Yuhuang, the Jade Emperor (left), was regarded as the most important of the gods, ruling a heaven staffed by a vast bureaucracy of lesser gods. The emperors of the Song dynasty (CE960–1279) encouraged the cult of Yuhuang in order to bolster their own imperial authority.

THE KITCHEN GOD

Tsao Chun was a good and honest mason, who was fated to remain poor all his life. The harder he worked, the poorer he became. At last his wife left him for another man. Unknowing, Tsao Chun contracted to work for this other man. His wife took pity on him, and baked him sesame cakes in which she hid money; but Tsao Chun, being fated to remain poor, gave the cakes away. When he found out what he had done, Tsao Chun killed himself. But Yuhuang, the Jade Emperor, took pity on him, and granted him eternal life as a kitchen god.

GODLY REPORTS

Announcements of village births and deaths were made at the temple of She Ji, the god of the ground and grain, who kept records of all that went on in the village, and reported them to heaven and hell.

Just as She Ji was thought to keep the gods informed about village life, a kitchen god, Tsao Chun, was thought to carry news of each household's doings to Yuhuang, the Jade Emperor, in heaven every New Year. The Chinese put Tsao Chun's printed image above their cooker. To make sure he said only good things, it was customary at New Year to spread honey on his mouth. The paper image was then burned to send it up to heaven, and a new print was put up.

Yuhuang was thought of as the divine equivalent of the emperor of China. He ruled over lesser gods, and kept track of each human life on earth. The news from She Ji and Tsao Chun helped in this vast task.

EVERY OBJECT HAS A SPIRIT

The Siberian province of Chukotka forms the northeastern tip of Asia. The indigenous peoples of Chukotka, such as the Chukchi, Koryak and Yupik (Siberian Inuit), share both the practical skills to survive in the treeless, snowbound wastes of this inhospitable landscape, and a mythology in which the spiritual and physical worlds are separated by only the thinnest of membranes.

The Chukchi never willingly submitted to the rule of the former Soviet Union. When in the 1930s they were instructed to collectivize their herds, many slaughtered their reindeer rather than abandon the old ways. There are around 15,000 Chukchi today. In the era of post-Soviet freedom, many of them are rediscovering the suppressed heritage of their traditional culture and mythology.

The Chukchi say that there was a single entrance to this world through the high mountains that surrounded it. People came into this world through the opening, until at last the cliffs snapped closed, breaking off one end of the kayak of the people just coming through. From that time, kayaks have only had one pointed end.

RAVEN'S ROCK

The Chukotka peoples believe that every object in the world has a spirit, which can act, speak and walk by itself; animals are believed to be able to change into human beings. Even today, after generations in which the native culture was suppressed and overlaid with that of Russia, Chukotka is a world of spirits and shamanism, alive with the magic of the creator Raven.

Over 100 years ago, the Chukchi said that Raven excreted the world. Now, this very raw and basic myth has been tidied up. Instead, Raven is said to have dropped a rock, which shattered to create the earth. But the essential story remains the same.

The name Chukchi comes from a word meaning 'rich in reindeer'. The Chukchi do not live in igloos like the Inuit, but in reindeer-hide tents called iarangas. Each family has its own tent, with the largest belonging to the owner of the reindeer herd, the Master of the Camp.

One Chukchi myth tells of two cousins. One of them lost his hunting skills, and was abandoned on an island. He was saved by a whale, which beached itself on the shore and died, giving him food. When his cousin returned he climbed out of his canoe, intrigued by the whale's skeleton. The abandoned man got into the canoe and rowed away, leaving his cousin to die instead.

Charms (whale amulet, above) were carved in the shape of the creatures that the Chukchi wished to have luck when hunting. A whale-shaped dish was carved for the altar at the annual Keretkun festival; it was filled with fresh water for the whale spirits to drink.

MARITIME RITUALS

The coastal peoples of Chukotka live by hunting the walrus, seals and whales of the Bering Sea. They believe that these creatures are the gift of the Master of the Sea – known to the Chukchi as Keretkun and to the Yupik as Kasak – or the Mistress of the Sea, Samna (the Yupik equivalent of the Inuit sea-goddess Sedna, see page 105). The Keretkun-Kasak festival at the end of autumn, in which the Master of the Sea was represented by a figurine and impersonated by a masked dancer, was formerly the chief ritual of the maritime Chukchi. It was designed to ensure continuing success in hunting for the coming year.

FROM THE FIRE

There once was a Chukchi woman whose husband died. She cut off his head and took it home, where it laughed all the time, causing her parents to throw her out. The head then told her to burn it on a fire of willow scrapings. From the fire stepped her husband, made new. The couple rose into the stars on a sleigh train drawn by reindeer stags, and lived in the world above. But every night when the woman saw her home again, she wept, and her tears became the rain.

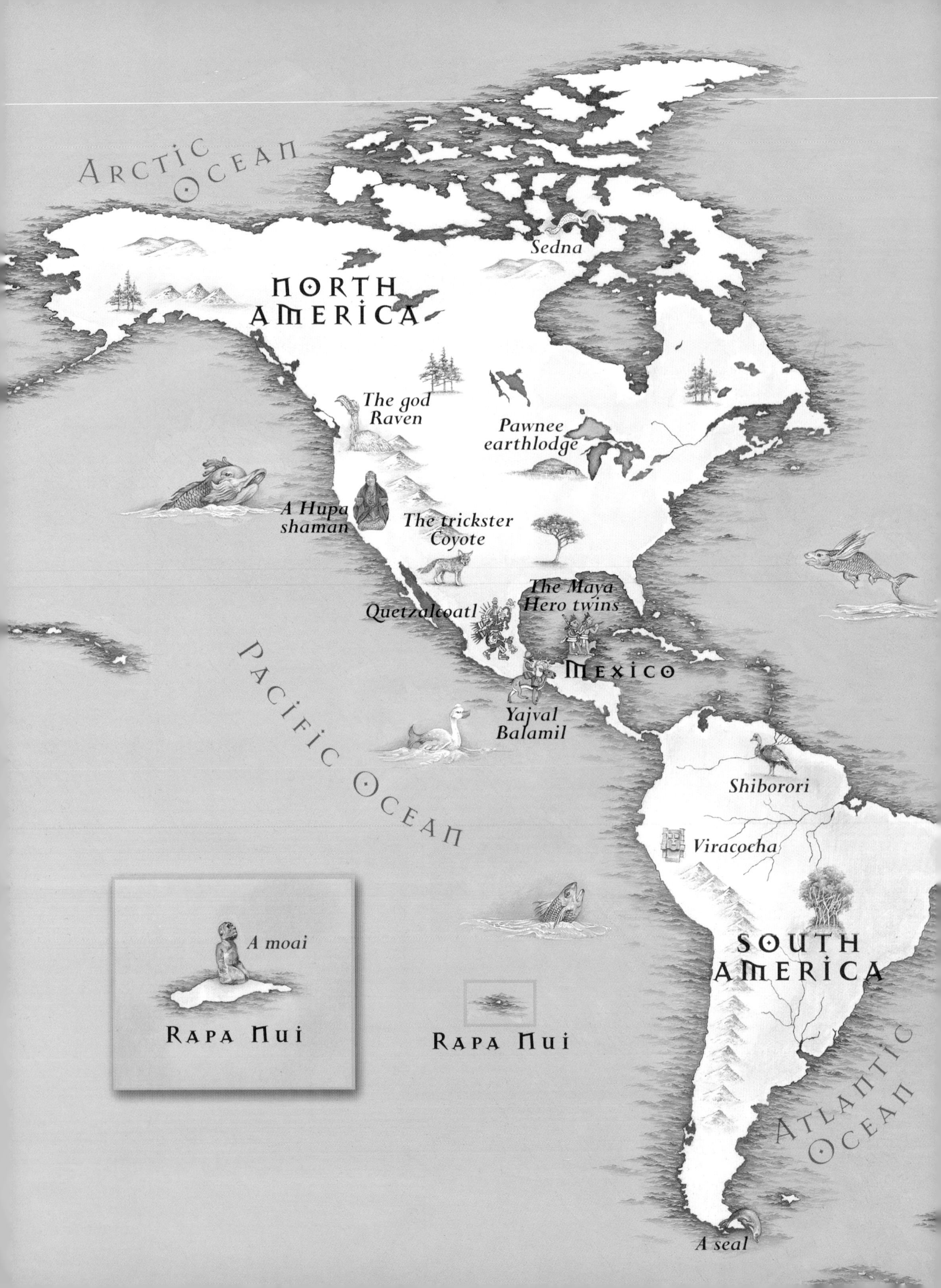

Arctic Ocean
Sedna
North America
The god Raven
Pawnee earthlodge
A Hupa shaman
The trickster Coyote
The Maya Hero twins
Quetzalcoatl
Mexico
Pacific Ocean
Yajval Balamil
Shiborori
Viracocha
South America
A moai
Rapa Nui
Rapa Nui
Atlantic Ocean
A seal

The Americas

The continents of North and South America – joined by the

narrow strip of land called Mesoamerica if it includes

Mexico – provide a wide variety of habitats, from the icy

Arctic to the heat of the Amazon rainforest. The myths of the

native peoples are equally varied. The First Nations of North

America divide geographically into ten main culture groups:

Northeast, Southeast, Plains, Southwest, California, Great

Basin, Plateau, Northwest Coast, Subarctic and Arctic. The

South American peoples fall into similar culture groups.

A WORLD DIVIDED

The Netsilingmiut – also known as the Netsilik Inuit – of the Canadian Arctic comprised a number of nomadic bands, each with their own hunting area, but with a common culture and mythology. Traditional Netsilingmiut life depended on the materials to be found in the frozen wastes of the Arctic: snow and ice to make igloos; caribou fur and sealskin to make clothes; and bone antlers to make tools and weapons.

The Netsilik believed that animals – as well as human beings – had undying souls, which must be appeased by special observances in the hunt. Hunters (Inuit hunter returning home, above) carried amulets believed to contain spirits that brought them luck in the chase and protected them against ghosts. The world was seen as full of dangerous spirits, the ghosts of humans or animals which had not obtained peace after death.

TRADITIONAL WAYS

The Netsilingmiut world was divided into two halves: the land and the sea. Traditionally, they lived entirely by hunting and fishing: hunting seals and other sea mammals in the winter and spring, and hunting caribou and other land animals in the summer and autumn. The Netsilingmiut did not have a hierarchical social structure with a headman; instead, the elders of each band discussed and agreed community matters informally. The Netsilingmiut people were also bound together by the strict etiquette of sharing meat from the hunt.

The Netsilingmiut angatkut, the great shamans, were believed to be protected by guardian spirits. Each angatkut could have a number of his own helpful guardian spirits.

Today, the Netsilingmiut are no longer nomadic hunters. Instead, they live in three permanent settlements – Taloyoak, Gjoa Haven and Kugaaruk – in Canada's newest territory, Nunavut, which means 'our land' in Netsilingmiut. They have government-supported schools, nursing stations, electricity and garbage disposal. Caribou are hunted by snowmobile, and handicrafts (hunt carving, above) are now an important source of income. Nunavut is nearly one-fifth the size of Canada.

Nuliayuk (above), who was also called Sedna, was an orphan girl who was thrown into the sea because no one cared about her. She tried to hang on to the kayak but the Inuit chopped off her fingers, which became the first seals, and she sank to the bottom of the sea.

ANIMAL LIVES

A long time ago, there was a great shaman who wanted to see what it was like to live the lives of all the animals. So he let himself be reborn as each animal. For a while he was a bear. That was a tiring life, for bears are always walking, even in the dark. Then he became a seal, and that was great fun, for seals are always playing in the waves; it is their high spirits that set the sea in motion. Next he became a wolf, and almost starved to death, until the other wolves took pity on him, and taught him how to run and to catch caribou. Then he turned into a musk ox, revelling in the warmth at the centre of the great herds. Finally he became a caribou, and was scared all the time. And so the shaman learned about all the animals, and taught his findings to the Netsilingmiut.

Netsilingmiut angatkuts (carving, right) mediated between the spirit world and the human world.

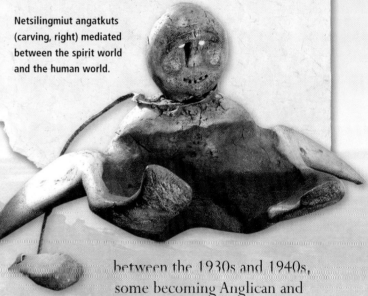

NETSILINGMIUT DEITIES

The Netsilingmiut had three main deities. Nuliayuk, who was also known as Sedna, mother of the sea beasts, lived at the bottom of the sea. Nârssuk, who was also known as Sila, the giant baby, was the master of the wind, snow and rain. Tatqiq, the moon man, was the hunter who fed the souls of the dead in the village of eternal homecoming in the sky. All of these gods were known by other Inuit groups.

The traditional life of the Netsilingmiut has radically changed over the last century, partly through government policies, and partly through the fur trade and missionary churches. Most Netsilingmiut converted to Christianity between the 1930s and 1940s, some becoming Anglican and others Roman Catholic. This led to a rejection of previous beliefs, including the intricate system of taboos that evolved from traditional Netsilingmiut belief in spirits and the spirit world. Shamanism died out as a result. But the increased welfare has reduced child mortality, and the Netsilik population has jumped from 259 in 1923 to over 2,000 today.

ANCESTORS

The Nuxalk Nation (also known as the Bella Coola) once occupied a number of permanent villages in the Bella Coola valley, in a rugged, mountainous area of British Columbia, 120km from the Pacific Ocean. They now live in a single village on the south shore of the Bella Coola river. Like other native American peoples of the northwest coast, they do not grow crops, but rely on fishing and hunting, and various wild plants.

The supreme god was Alquntam (left), who created four carpenters to carve the geographical features of the world, the flowers and animals, and finally the first human beings. These humans then each chose a bird or animal 'cloak' from those hanging in the House of Myths, and descended to earth in that form.

SHARING WEALTH

The Nuxalk had a particularly rich ceremonial life. One important custom was the potlatch, a ceremony at which a chief would prove his status by giving away valuable goods. The first potlatches were held by the mythical ancestors, after they came down to earth, to demonstrate how well they had prospered in the Nuxalk country. Potlatches were outlawed between 1884 and 1951 by the Canadian government, who believed that this custom prevented the Nuxalk from becoming 'civilized'. This anti-potlatch law caused a break in the continuity of Nuxalk culture.

Nuxalk houses are built from planks of red cedar (background), and often stand on stilts as a defence against flooding. The front of the house is usually decorated with the owner's 'crest', an image of the animal form of the earliest family ancestor. The origin myths of these first ancestors, who came down to earth in animal form, bind the Nuxalk into a number of ancestral families.

Raven steals the sun

At the beginning of time, Alquntam created the forefathers of humankind in the House of Myths, and asked each of them in what form they wished to descend to earth. The cleverest of them all chose the form of a raven.

When the forefathers reached earth, they were horrified to discover how dark it was; there was just a glimmer of light like pale moonlight. Luckily, Raven remembered that he had once seen the sun in the House of Myths. He flew back up in his raven form, and then changed himself into a speck of dust, settling in the cup of Alquntam's daughter. But the girl blew away the dust. Then Raven turned himself into a smear of mud on the water. This time it worked, and she drank the water, and Raven, from the cup.

In the course of time, Alquntam's daughter gave birth to a baby boy, who was actually Raven, reborn as a child. Within a few weeks, Raven had grown into a naughty little boy. One day, he saw the sun hanging up in the roof, only dimly gleaming because it was kept inside a container. He demanded the shiny thing to play with. As soon as he had it, Raven rolled it out of the door. As the sun rolled outside, it collided with the doorpost, bursting the container that had dimmed its light. Raven the child then transformed into a raven and flew off with the sun.

Some Nuxalk acquired the power to heal the sick and became shamans (statue of a Nuxalk shaman, left). A select few received their knowledge directly from Alquntam. One shaman-to-be scalded himself when cooking and was told by Alquntam of the imminent coming of the white men, with their wonderful cooking pots and their houses that would stay warm without the need of a fire.

A unique culture

Over the last century, the economic focus of Nuxalk society has changed. The main occupations are now commercial fishing and logging. At the same time, the large old dwellings that housed extended families have been replaced by modern homes for individual families. Most of the Nuxalk have now converted to Methodist Christianity, but they retain an intimate link to their traditonal beliefs. The Nuxalk were never removed from their ancestral lands, and since the 1960s there has been an active revival of Nuxalk traditions. According to myth, when a Nuxalk dies, his or her spirit retraces the path of the ancestors and rises to live in the House of Myths.

WORLD RENEWAL

The Hupa live in Hoopa Valley in northwestern California. Many of the First Nations of northern California, such as the Yana, suffered genocide at the hands of white settlers at the time of the California Gold Rush in the 1850s. Luckily, there was little gold on the Hupa land, and in 1864 Congress set aside almost the whole of the Hupa territory as a reservation.

Most Hupa shamans were women. The shaman acquired her healing powers by swallowing a 'pain', and learning to control it to cure others. All illnesses were thought to be caused by these semi-animate pains, which the shaman sucked from the patient's body, and captured in basketwork cups.

The Hupa lived on fish from the Trinity river (man spearing salmon, below) and on acorns and other plant foods harvested from the forest.

SYMBOLS OF WEALTH

The Hupa, unlike most native Californian peoples, defined social status by wealth. Besides a kind of money made from dentalium (mollusc) shell, they valued rare items such as the skin of an albino deer or a scarlet-feathered woodpecker. At the great annual festival of the White Deerskin Dance, participants displayed these symbols of wealth. Women's deerskin dance skirts were richly decorated with beading, and hung with tinkling brass bells. The Deerskin Dance lasted ten days. Its purpose was 'world renewal'.

Until 1850 the Hupa remained in relative seclusion. At that time the Hupa population was around 1,000. This figure was halved in the following half century, but reached again in the 1960s. Today, there are over 2,000 Hupa living as a self-governing people in the 35,200-hectare Hoopa Valley Reservation, which has always been the centre of the Hupa world.

The Hupa live in permanent houses built of cedar planks. Woodwork in cedar is the main male craft, for wood is plentiful on the mountains surrounding Hoopa Valley, with their evergreen forests of cedar, pine and Douglas fir. Today, much of the wealth of the Hupa nation comes from logging.

THE KIXUNAI

An important part of the Deerskin Dance was the recounting of myths telling how the rituals were established in the creation time by the Kixunai, the first people. By re-telling the myths, the Hupa tapped into the powers of creation to revitalize the world for the coming year. The effect was to wipe away the evil brought on the world by those who had transgressed one of the many taboos that dominated Hupa life.

SACRED BASKETS

One day, a Kixunai girl sat on the edge of the ocean with her legs in the water. She was weaving a basket, and singing as she worked. The wind was blowing gently from the north. As she sang, the wind grew fiercer, until a great gust came and blew the basket away. She tried to retrieve it from the water, but she could not. The next day the girl went down to the beach and found the basket floating in the shallows. When she took it out of the water it was covered with clinging dentalia*. It had floated all around the world, to every place where the dentalia grew. After that, all her baskets attracted wealth.

'I have done this for the Hupa women who will come afterwards,' the Kixunai girl said. 'I wish long life for the woman who always has a basket in her hands.'

* Dentalia are molluscs whose shells were used as currency by the Hupa. Dentalium shells were valued by their length, which Hupa men measured against a series of marks tattooed on the left forearm.

Hupa women prayed to the Kixunai girl from the basket myth to loan them her magic powers while they wove their baskets. Hupa baskets were woven using hazel shoots for the warp and filaments of tree root for the weft. Patterns were added by overlaying black and dyed-red fern stems.

STAR CHILDREN

The Pawnee were one of the largest of the buffalo-hunting nations of America's Great Plains. Their territory was in central Nebraska and northern Kansas. At the turn of the 18th century CE, they numbered over 10,000. Two centuries later, the population was 500, reduced by disease, warfare and the 1876 removal of the people to new land in the Oklahoma Indian Territory. Today, they number about 2,500.

Hunting and farming formed a yearly cycle of activities for the Pawnee (above). The communal summer hunt began after the second hoeing of the corn in early July, and ended in the autumn. The winter hunt began in November, and lasted until spring.

SACRED BUNDLES

A unique feature of Pawnee mythology was its emphasis on the stars. The Pawnee believed that they were made by the stars, and that at the end of the world, they themselves would turn into stars. The supreme creator was Tirawahat, the expanse of the heavens. Other important deities were Sun, Moon and Evening Star.

Each village had a creation myth that told how its founder was created by a star, and given a sacred bundle containing his power. This sacred bundle was passed down by each chief to his son, so that each new chief was regarded as a descendant of the founder. The bundle in turn was a source of supernatural power to which the entire village had access. The protection of this bundle was the first duty of the village.

TRADITIONAL CULTURE

The priests were the link between the human and supernatural worlds. They performed an annual cycle of rituals to the star deities, starting with the Creation Ritual of the Evening Star Bundle, which was held in the spring.

In addition to the priests, there were also secret medicine societies, whose doctors had the power to cure the sick and perform miracles.

By 1891, much of the traditional Pawnee culture had disappeared. The last priests who knew the great rituals had died. Instead, many of the remaining Pawnee embraced a new religion, the Ghost Dance. This led to a brief revival of the old rituals and dances, but by 1930 this came to an end. The last speakers of the Pawnee language died in the 1990s.

The Pawnee lived in earthlodge villages along the Platte and Loup rivers. Each earthlodge housed between 30 and 50 people, divided into two groups, the north side and the south side, which alternated the daily chores. The lodges were left empty during the winter hunt, and often had to be rebuilt in the spring. The lodge design followed the pattern laid down by the creator Tirawahat in the beginning.

Today, Pawnee dances are social occasions with none of their former religious significance. Most Pawnees belong to the Indian Methodist and Indian Baptist churches, although some belong to the native American churches, which arose from the Ghost Dance and Peyote religions.

TIRAWAHAT

After Tirawahat had created the sun, moon, stars and earth, he spoke, and at the sound of his voice a woman appeared on earth. Tirawahat asked the other gods in the heavens what to do to make the woman happy. They advised him to create a man to keep her company through life. He told the man and woman that they must call the earth 'mother' and the sky 'father'.

Then he showed them how to make an earthlodge, with four posts holding up the lodge, much like the four gods who hold up the heavens. Each pole was to represent a different god, and the entrance was always to be in the east, to allow the lodge to breathe as if it were a human. In the very centre of the lodge was the fireplace, and in the west, an altar with a buffalo skull. The spirit of Tirawahat would enter the skull when the first rays of sun shone on it in the morning.

Tirawahat then gave the man and woman the first sacred bundle to hang above the altar. He also taught them ceremonies and dances, and showed them how to grow corn and how to call to the buffalo.

Siuuhu's Revenge

The Akimel O'odham, which means the 'river people', make up a native American nation of southern Arizona and northern Sonora, Mexico. Today, about 15,000 Akimel O'odham, also known as the Pima, live along rivers in the Sonoran desert.

Siuuhu and Jewed Ma:kai created the sun, the moon and the stars, the clouds and rain, people and animals. From the sun and the moon, the trickster Coyote was born. Many archaeologists believe that one of the gigantic figures (above) at Blythe, on the California-Arizona border, represents Siuuhu.

The Akimel O'odham (right) adapted so well to their desert environment that it has created a serious health problem for contemporary Akimel O'odham. Now that they live a less active lifestyle, and eat a rich western diet, about half of all adults develop diabetes, at the average age of 36. It seems that there is probably a genetic cause, linked to the previous need to store fat to survive in a hostile, water-deprived environment.

Only archaeological remnants of the Hohokam civilization remain, such as the system of canal irrigation, which is still in the valley of the Salt river (above).

THOSE WHO HAVE GONE

The Sonoran desert is a hostile environment, for both water and food are in very short supply. But along the rivers, where wild plants and animals are most abundant, the Akimel O'odham established permanent villages. Farming the alluvial flood plains, they made the desert bloom. According to their mythology, they were taught how to farm and to irrigate the land, by the god Siuuhu, the elder brother.

The Akimel O'odham believe they are the descendants of the pre-Columbian Hohokam. Some of their villages were built on the sites of Hohokam ruins. But many scholars think there was a gap between the decline of the 1,000-year-old Hohokam civilization (whose classic period ended around CE 1450) and the rise of the Akimel O'odham.

Since 1934, when the Indian Reorganization Act gave the Akimel O'odham the ability to shape their future, there has been an increase in prosperity. Today, the Akimel O'odham live in concrete houses, drive trucks and operate modern businesses. But they have not abandoned their traditional ways of thinking: they still believe in co-operation in search of 'lasting well-being'.

BACK TO LIFE

The Akimel O'odham mythological cycle began with the creation of the universe by Jewed Ma:kai, the earth doctor, and ended with the vanquishing of the Hohokam and the establishment of the Akimel O'odham villages. According to an Akimel O'odham myth, the Hohokam were conquered because they killed the god who had made them.

Siuuhu, the god the Hohokam killed, came back to life and summoned the Akimel O'odham from the underworld to avenge his death. The ancestors of the Akimel O'odham had fled to the underworld to escape the flood that ended the first age of the world. Now they could return to their homeland.

The lands of the Akimel O'odham were transferred in 1853 from Mexico to the USA, and entered a period of catastrophe. White settlers reduced the Akimel O'odham from independent farmers to wage labourers, and from prosperity to poverty. Their traditional culture was eroded, and many Akimel O'odham were converted to Presbyterian Christianity (church, right).

A DEAD ARMY

A time came when the Hohokam people began to feel superior to Siuuhu, who had created them from clay. When Ñu:wi, the buzzard, came to them, and offered to kill Siuuhu, they agreed.

Ñu:wi flew up to the sun and borrowed the sun's bow. He then shot Siuuhu with a sun-ray arrow. Siuuhu felt his heart growing hotter and hotter. And then he fell down dead.

Siuuhu lay dead for four years until Jewed Ma:kai sent the four winds to nurse him back to life. When Siuuhu recovered, he went down to the underworld and led an army of the Akimel O'odham dead from the underworld. The Akimel O'odham vanquished the Hohokam and took their place on earth.

Heroic Tales

The Maya civilization in the Yucatán Peninsula, Mexico, and in the highlands of Guatemala, was past its peak by the 16th century CE, when the arrival of the Spanish conquerors brought the Catholic religion to replace the Maya gods. But the Maya survived and today number around five million people.

The Maya Hero Twins Hunahpu and Xbalanque descended to the underworld to avenge their father and uncle, who had been sacrificed by the lords of Xibalba and buried beneath the ball court. The twins successfully vanquished the lords of death.

The sacred ball game was played in a ball court which was a narrow alley between two stands (below). The players batted a solid rubber ball with their upper arm, aiming it towards various markers. It was half-sport, half-ritual. The ball represented the sun, on its journey in and out of the underworld. Sometimes the victorious players cut the heads off the losing ones, storing their skulls in special racks behind the ball court. Carvings of the ball game at Chichén Itzá (left) show a skull on the surface of the ball.

Telling the Time

The civilization of the Maya developed slowly over the first millennium BCE, and reached its classical peak in the 3rd century CE. Theirs was a culture based on dynastic rule in city-states, with phonetic writing and a complex calendar with a number of different ways of telling the time.

By CE 900, the greatest city of the Maya was at Chichén Itzá in northern Yucatán, but this, like earlier cities, gradually declined. By the time the Spanish arrived, the Maya in both Yucatán and the Guatemalan highlands had fragmented from a great united empire into a collection of smaller peoples.

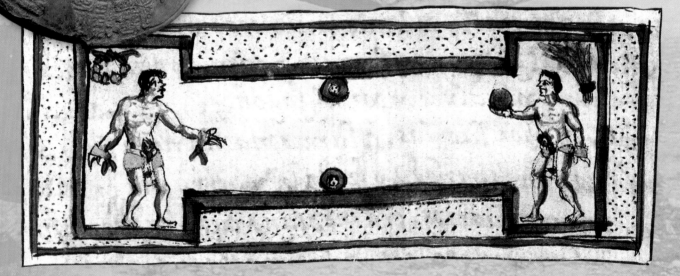

THE MAYA MINDSET

The Quiché Maya of Guatemala were conquered by the Spanish in 1524. Afterwards, one Quiché nobleman had his people's sacred book, the Popol Vuh, transcribed from Maya hieroglyphs into the European alphabet, and it is this book above all that allows us to understand the mythology and the mindset of the Maya.

The Popol Vuh is a mythological history of the world. The first part tells of the creation of the earth, the animals and the first people. The second follows the adventures of the mythical Hero Twins Hunahpu and Xbalanque; and the third tells of the creation from maize of the four founding fathers of the Quiché lineages, and lists 14 generations of their descendants down to the middle of the 16th century CE.

GREAT EXPLOITS

The Hero Twins lived in a time of darkness, under the rule of the monstrous bird Vucub Caquix, the false sun. They shot him down with their blowguns, clearing the way for the true sun to rise. Vucub Caquix is thought to be the principal bird deity, a god represented in Maya carvings as early as 300BCE.

The second great exploit of the Hero Twins is their descent to the underworld, where they overcame the lords of Xibalba (death). The story begins with the sacred ball game, which was played all over Central America and prehispanic Mexico. This game was connected to ideas about human sacrifice, which was required by the gods in return for the gift of fire.

SO MANY HOUSES

The Hero Twins Hunahpu and Xbalanque were challenged by the dreadful lords of Xibalba, the underworld, to a game of tlachtli, the Mayan ritual ball game. When they won, they were thrown into the House of Lances, where they were stabbed by demons. They escaped, but were imprisoned in turn in the Houses of Cold, Jaguars, Fire and Bats. The Hero Twins survived all these and, boasting that they were immortal, had themselves sacrificed and their bones ground to flour. Then the Hero Twins came back to life. The lords of Xibalba were so impressed that they wanted to die and be reborn themselves.

'Do it to us!' begged the lords of Xibalba. So the Hero Twins killed the lords of death; but they did not revive them.

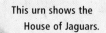

This urn shows the House of Jaguars.

BLOOD-SOAKED GIFTS

The Aztecs were a related group of Nahuatl-speaking tribes, rather than a single people, living in the Valley of Mexico from the 12th century CE. The most powerful of these tribes was the Mexica, who ruled the Aztec empire – which came to encompass most of central and southern Mexico – from what is today Mexico City, until the coming of the Spanish conquerors in 1519.

When Cortés arrived in 1519 (left), it is estimated that there were between 20 and 25 million people in Mexico. By the end of the century, war and disease had reduced the population to one million, and this together with forced conversion from the Aztec religion to Catholicism destroyed Aztec civilization.

The Aztecs fed Huitzilopochtli's (above) hunger for still-beating hearts by practising a kind of warfare known as 'flowery war', in which the object was not to win a victory, but to capture as many as possible of the enemy as sacrificial victims. This strange style of war turned out to be utterly unsuitable to counter the efficient European warfare of the Spanish.

GRUESOME SACRIFICE

Aztec culture is linked to earlier Mesoamerican civilizations such as the Olmecs (from 1200BCE), the Zapotecs (from 600BCE), the Teotihuacanos (from CE100), the Toltecs (from CE900), and of course the Maya (see pages 114–115). Inheriting a rich mythology from this past, the Aztecs gave it a brutal twist by insisting on the worship of the sun god Huitzilopochtli, who demanded a regular sacrifice of still-beating human hearts.

One of the main roles of Quetzalcoatl (right) was that of wind god. The Aztecs believed that the sun only moved because it was blown by Quetzalcoatl's breath. He also acted as road-sweeper for the life-giving rain gods, such as Tlaloc, whose rain made the maize grow.

Blood and bones

After the flood that ended the fourth sun, or fourth age, Quetzalcoatl and his brother, Tezcatlipoca, created the new heaven and earth. Then Quetzalcoatl descended to Mictlan, the underworld, to steal the bones of humankind from his father, Mictlantecuhtli, the god of death. Quetzalcoatl persuaded his father into giving up the bones, but Mictlantecuhtli did not really want to let them go, so he asked the ghosts of the underworld to dig a hole, into which Quetzalcoatl fell, scattering the bones all around.

A quail nibbled the bones where they lay, and because of this the new race that Quetzalcoatl created was doomed to die again. Quetzalcoatl then ground the bones like corn, into a fine meal, into which he spilled his own blood, thus creating the present race of human beings*.

*This was why the Aztecs believed they owed a blood debt to their creator Quetzalcoatl. When they initially thought Cortés was Quetzalcoatl, they offered him maize cakes soaked in human blood, as food fit for a god.

The Aztec god of death, Mictlantecuhtli, was depicted as a skeleton (right), often with spots of red blood on his white bones. With his wife Mictecacihuatl, he ruled the underworld of Mictlan. They were the parents of Quetzalcoatl, the god of life.

A fatal error

The Aztecs worshipped a great many gods and goddesses, but one of the most important was Quetzalcoatl, the feathered serpent. He was half-rattlesnake and half-quetzal bird. Quetzalcoatl pre-dated the Aztecs, and seems to have been worshipped by earlier civilizations from around 1200 BCE.

According to an Aztec myth, it was Quetzalcoatl who gave the gift of corn to men, and also taught them many arts and sciences. He had one great rival – his own brother, Tezcatlipoca, a god of war and sorcery. Tezcatlipoca tricked Quetzalcoatl into getting drunk. Ashamed of himself, Quetzalcoatl sailed away east on a raft of serpents, promising to return to the Aztecs one day.

Quetzalcoatl was a god, but he also had a human incarnation as king of the legendary city of Tollan. All Aztec kings modelled themselves on Quetzalcoatl, and awaited his return.

One of the most distinguishing features of Quetzalcoatl was his conical hat, which was echoed in the conical roof of his temple at Tenochtitlan, in the Valley of Mexico. Hernán Cortés (1485–1547), leader of the Spanish army, also wore a high-crowned hat. When Cortés landed in 1519, the Aztecs made the error of assuming him to be the returning god (see page 120 for a similar event concerning the Incas).

117

Maya descendants

The Tzotzil people, modern descendants of the Maya (see pages 114–115), live in the highlands of Chiapas in southern Mexico. In this mountainous region there are fertile upland valleys at about 2,100m above sea level, and in one of these valleys is the 117km² municipality of Zinacantán, consisting of a ceremonial centre and 15 hamlets, home to about 12,000 Tzotzil-speaking Zinacantecs.

The hamlets of the Zinacantec are scattered among the upland valleys and limestone and volcanic mountains of the Chiapas highlands. Because of the long dry season from October to May, access to water is vital for the survival of both humans and animals, so hamlets are often called after their sacred waterholes, such as Vo'cho'oh Vo', the five waterholes.

It is believed that baptism 'fixes' the inner soul in the body, but some parts of it are still easily lost at moments of excitement or fright. Therefore, a Zinacantec mother away from home will always sweep the ground on which her infant has been sitting with her shawl (traditional Zinacantec weaving, below), making sure to gather up any stray parts of the child's soul.

The navel of the world

The Zinacantecs have a unique culture that blends their Maya past, their four centuries under Spanish rule, and the realities of life today. They believe the world is a cube, resting on the shoulders of the Four-Corner gods. At the centre of the upper surface of this cube is the navel of the world – a low mound of earth in the ceremonial centre of Zinacantán, the site of a shrine where Zinacantecs pray and make offerings.

The Zinacantecs believe that Father Sun circles the world, preceded by the Morning Star, the sweeper of the path. At noon, Father Sun pauses in his travels to look down at the Zinacantecs to see what they are doing, and then continues on his way. So most Zinacantec rituals are conducted facing the east, where the sun rises.

Mules and money

A man was sheltering from the rain when Yajval Balamil came up from below to see who had come into his cave. Sometimes brave men enter his caves and he rewards them with money or livestock; sometimes they are not so lucky, for Yajval Balamil always needs workers to look after his herds of mules. Yajval Balamil gave this man nothing but a pair of iron sandals, saying, 'You must work for me until these sandals are worn out.'

So the man became a muleteer under the earth. He worked there for three years. When he got home, his wife would not believe his story, until eight mule loads of money arrived – his pay from Yajval Balamil.

The Zinacantecs celebrate many saints' days with three-day fiestas. At midnight on Christmas Eve in the church of San Sebastian, they re-enact the birth of the two Christ children (an older and a younger brother in Zinacantec belief), and then carry the two children to an elaborate crèche erected the previous day in the church of San Lorenzo.

Mountain ancestors

The mountains and hills around Zinacantán are the homes of the ancestral gods, who are remote ancestors to whom the Zinacantecs pray and make offerings of black chickens, candles, incense and rum. These ancestral gods are thought of as being like elderly Zinacantecs, who were established inside the mountains by the Four-Corner gods to be the watchful guardians of Zinacantec lore and culture. Only Zinacantec shamans, who are called by a series of dreams, can see into the mountains and communicate directly with the ancestral gods.

Outwardly, Zinacantán appears devoutly Catholic, for it has hundreds of wooden crosses and cross shrines. But although all Zinacantecs are baptized into the Catholic church, the overlay of Christianity across older Maya beliefs can be thin. Crosses by caves or waterholes are conceived as channels of communication with Yajval Balamil, the earth owner, a powerful god who must be placated before any work is done on the land, and the kalvarios, the cross shrines, are meeting places of the ancestral gods.

Maize plants, the most important crop for the Zinacantecs, are called 'the sunbeams of the gods', and are believed to have an inner soul, just like a human being. The human inner soul, located in the heart, is believed to have 13 separate parts. If one of these is lost, a person must undergo a special curing ceremony to recover it. The shaman uses 13 grains of maize – white, yellow, red and black – to divine which pieces of the soul are missing.

119

GODS AND GOLD

Tawantinsuyu, the Inca empire, spread from Ecuador in the north, through Peru, Chile and southeastern Bolivia to northeastern Argentina. Founded in the Peruvian city of Cuzco around CE1200, the Inca dynasty inherited the cultural achievements and the mythology of a series of pre-Inca civilizations that stretched back 2,000 years.

In the Temple of the Sun (ruins, above), there was a wonderful gold image of the sun god Inti, showing him as a human face surrounded by sun rays. The worship of Inti was a specifically Inca, rather than a pan-Andean, cult.

The belief that Manco Capac, the first Inca king, was the earthly manifestation of the sun secured the Inca king's right to rule. But there was a counter-myth that claimed Manco Capac was an imposter, just like Pizarro (above).

PLAYING GOD

The classic Inca period lasted less than 100 years, from the time they swept over South America subduing many other peoples, and making them subject to the Inca king, to the moment the Inca empire collapsed after the arrival of the Spanish adventurer Francisco Pizarro (1475–1541) in 1532. That Pizarro and a force of 180 men could overthrow a military empire of several millions is one of history's most extraordinary stories, and it is one that is only explained by reference to mythology. For the last Inca emperor Atahuallpa (c.1502–1533) – who had just fought and won a bloody civil war against his half-brother Huascar (d.1533) – was anticipating the prophesied return across the sea of the creator god Viracocha. When he heard of the Spaniards' landing, he assumed that this was in fact Viracocha and his sons. By the time he understood his mistake, Atahuallpa was Pizarro's prisoner, and the Spaniards had taken over Cuzco, the city that controlled the Inca empire.

Atahuallpa (left) believed that as a direct descendant of the sun god he ruled by divine right. The emperor was the 'son of the sun', the Incas were the 'children of the sun', and the gold was the 'sweat of the sun'.

120

VIRACOCHA WALKS ON WATER

Viracocha was the creator of earth and time. He emerged from Lake Titicaca in the primeval darkness and created a race of giants. But they angered him, and he sent a flood that drowned them and turned them to stone; their statues can still be seen at Tiahuanaco, near the lake. So Viracocha summoned the sun, the moon and the stars to come forth from the Island of the Sun in the centre of the lake. Then he took stones that were lying along the shore and moulded them into the shape of human beings. He painted these models with the clothes they were to wear, and gave each group its own language, songs and seeds to plant for food. Viracocha and his sons went among the people, instructing them how to live, and then set off across the Pacific Ocean, walking on the waves, leaving the people to wait for their promised return.

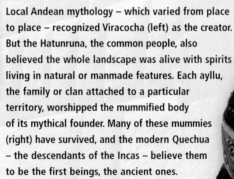

Local Andean mythology – which varied from place to place – recognized Viracocha (left) as the creator. But the Hatunruna, the common people, also believed the whole landscape was alive with spirits living in natural or manmade features. Each ayllu, the family or clan attached to a particular territory, worshipped the mummified body of its mythical founder. Many of these mummies (right) have survived, and the modern Quechua – the descendants of the Incas – believe them to be the first beings, the ancient ones.

TREASURE HUNT

It was the lure of gold that drew Pizarro to Peru. When Atahuallpa understood that, he offered to fill his prison cell with gold objects, higher than a man could reach, in return for his freedom. Pizarro agreed. The Temple of the Sun in Cuzco was stripped of its gold, then llama trains began arriving from all over the empire, laden with gold treasures. When the cell was full, the Spaniards gathered up the treasures and melted them down into gold bars.

As for Atahuallpa, all his gold could not buy his life. He was condemned to be burned alive. As the wood was about to be lit, he was told that if he accepted Christianity, his sentence would be changed to garrotting. So he was baptised, and then strangled.

WATERWORLD

The Warao have lived since prehistoric times in the remote tidal swamps of the Orinoco delta on the east coast of Venezuela. Their name means 'boat people', and their dugout canoes are central both to their daily life and to their mythology. These canoes embody the spirit of Dauarani, the mother of the forest.

The delicate ecology of the Orinoco delta has provided the Warao with a unique way of life. This eco-niche is now under threat from oil exploration by multinational companies, which the Warao – who today number about 25,000 – are determined to fight off.

DREAMING OF BOATS

The skill of the Warao boat-builders has been renowned for centuries, and was mentioned as early as 1596 by Sir Walter Raleigh (1552–1618). The worst thing you can say about a Warao man is that he has no canoe. Fathers carve toy canoes for their infant children so that each child can sit and paddle on imaginary journeys; by the age of three, all Warao children can manage a real canoe perfectly. The Warao virtually live in their cachicamo-tree canoes and, when they die, they are buried in them.

A boat-maker is called to the craft by a dream vision that binds him to the service of Dauarani, who was herself born from the first canoe. Each boat he builds recreates his vision, and the slow process of creating a new canoe is, for the builder, a mystical search for spiritual bliss, as well as a practical exercise.

The Warao live in a watery world, criss-crossed by a network of drainage rivers and waterways that divide the land into innumerable islands. The Orinoco delta is flat, so the Warao always see the world from sea level. From this viewpoint, the world looks like a narrow band between the water and the sky, and this is how the Warao imagine the earth, as a thin flat disc surrounded by water.

LEAVING THE TREES

In the beginning, the Warao lived in the treetops, jumping from one tree to another, and eating fruits and birds. One day, a hunter shot a bird that was so heavy it crashed right through the thick canopy of leaves, and opened up a passage to the ground below. Climbing down to collect the bird, the hunter was amazed to find himself standing on the ground. The Warao had no idea it was there.

'Come down,' he shouted to the others. 'Here is a place to put your feet. It is large, and it is surrounded by water.'

And ever since, the Warao have called the earth Hobahi, or that which is surrounded by water. But some of those who lived in the treetops did not want to come down; they turned into evil spirits.

BABIES AND GODS

Warao mythology tells of various gods, the Ancient Ones, who live on sacred mountains at the four corners of the earth, with the Warao living at the very centre. These gods depend on human beings to nourish them with offerings, especially tobacco; in turn, the Warao depend on the gods for health and life.

But neither can be taken for granted by the Warao, who today are plagued by western illnesses such as tuberculosis. Although modern medicines are improving matters, it is hard to provide medical aid in the inaccessible maze of waterways in which the Warao live.

When a baby is born, it enters a lifelong bond with the Warao gods. The baby's very first cry carries across the world to the mountain home of

Until recently the Warao suffered 49 per cent infant mortality. These children were said to be claimed as food by the spirits of the underworld. Those who survived did so under the supernatural protection of Shiborori, the mythical bird of beautiful plumage (represented by the ocellated turkey, left), seen in dreams and visions by the Warao priest-shamans, the Masters of Pain.

Ariawara, the god of origin, in the east, and the god's own welcoming cry echoes back. On the third day after a baby is born, Hahuba, the snake of being, sends a balmy breeze to the village, to embrace the new arrival. Already, the baby is part of the balance between natural and supernatural that forms Warao daily life.

No more stories

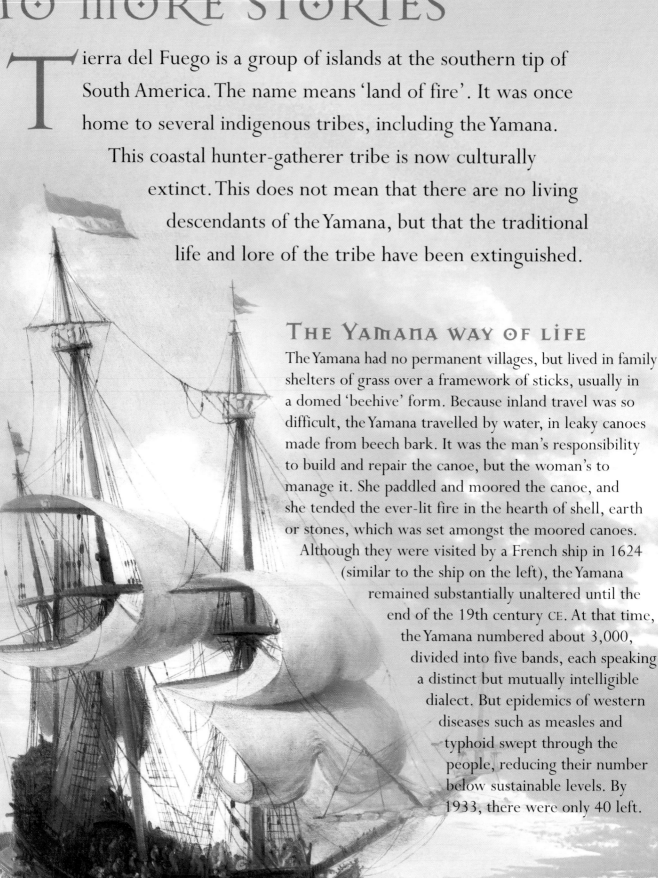

Tierra del Fuego is a group of islands at the southern tip of South America. The name means 'land of fire'. It was once home to several indigenous tribes, including the Yamana. This coastal hunter-gatherer tribe is now culturally extinct. This does not mean that there are no living descendants of the Yamana, but that the traditional life and lore of the tribe have been extinguished.

THE YAMANA WAY OF LIFE

The Yamana had no permanent villages, but lived in family shelters of grass over a framework of sticks, usually in a domed 'beehive' form. Because inland travel was so difficult, the Yamana travelled by water, in leaky canoes made from beech bark. It was the man's responsibility to build and repair the canoe, but the woman's to manage it. She paddled and moored the canoe, and she tended the ever-lit fire in the hearth of shell, earth or stones, which was set amongst the moored canoes. Although they were visited by a French ship in 1624 (similar to the ship on the left), the Yamana remained substantially unaltered until the end of the 19th century CE. At that time, the Yamana numbered about 3,000, divided into five bands, each speaking a distinct but mutually intelligible dialect. But epidemics of western diseases such as measles and typhoid swept through the people, reducing their number below sustainable levels. By 1933, there were only 40 left.

The Yamana – their own name for themselves, which means 'human beings' – lived mostly on the coast. Here, there was abundant food such as mussels, fish and seals in the sea, while the mountainous and heavily wooded interiors of the islands were difficult to penetrate, and contained little game. Long evenings around a campfire were enlivened by the telling of traditional myths.

TRIBAL MYTHS

As the younger members of the Yamana embraced modern life, the older members, who still remembered the myths and wisdom of the tribe, refused to pass on the stories.

When storytelling, the Yamana constantly interwove their own personal experience with the adventures of the mythical ancestors. This brought the characters in the myths into the dramatic present, and at the same time allowed the myth-teller to show off.

But by the 1920s, the tribe no longer functioned as a traditional community with a shared culture and knowledge. The context in which this kind of storytelling made sense was gone. Without the stories, a culture that had survived for thousands of years fell into complete disintegration.

In marriage, the man was considered to be the head of the family, and in a society without chiefs, social classes or political structures, his authority was absolute. The central myth of the Yamana explained how this came about. In the beginning, the primeval ancestors such as Sun, Moon and Rainbow came to the Yamana country from the east, in human-animal form, and settled at a place called Yáiaasága. There, the women ruled over the men, until the men realized that they were being tricked, and seized control and power for themselves.

A CLEVER TRICK

When the first ancestors of the Yamana settled in Yáiaasága, the women were in charge. The men had to keep the fire going, look after the children and do everything they were told. Each day, the women would go into their kina, a large hut, and scream and shout as though frightened to death. Then the 'spirits' they had raised would come out of the hut and terrify the men.

But one day, Lem, the sun-man, was out hunting, when he came across two girls practising how to paint their bodies and put on masks to act the part of the spirits. He understood then that it had all been a trick to frighten the men.

The men were furious when Lem told them, and they rose up against the women. After a fierce battle, all the women were transformed into animals of land and sea. During the battle, the kina had caught fire. When Lem poured water on it, he created a mighty wave. As the wave rolled out to sea, it took the sea animals with it. Then Lem went up into the sky, where he became Sun. His brother Akáinix became Rainbow, and the former leader of the women, Hánuxa, became Moon.

An isolated island

If any place on earth deserves the title 'the middle of nowhere', it is the tiny Pacific island of Rapa Nui, also called Easter island. It is over 2,000km from its nearest neighbour, Pitcairn island. Though it belongs to Chile, it was settled not from South America but from Polynesia, sometime around the 7th century CE.

Rapa Nui lies in the Pacific Ocean, the largest and deepest of the world's oceans. The island has no rivers or streams – a feature that dismayed Hoto Matu'a when he arrived. His descendants had to adapt their skills in woodcarving to stone, because Rapa Nui lacked suitable trees, and the volcanic tuff (stone) was light and easy to carve.

The moai (below) are not gods; their oval eyes show that they represent human beings. Gods, such as Makemake, have round eyes. Instead, the statues are memorials to great chiefs.

The descendants of Hoto Matu'a

Hoto Matu'a, the great parent, the leader of the first settlers on Rapa Nui, was chief of an island far to the west. When his tattooer, Haumaka, dreamed of a land across the sea, Hoto Matu'a decided to sail there. All the ariki-mau, the great chiefs who are sometimes called kings, are descended from Hoto Matu'a, and claim his power to make Rapa Nui fertile. Their genealogies show a direct link between the ariki-mau and the gods, for the early names include those of such powerful Polynesian deities as Tangaroa, the sea god, and Rongo, the god of agriculture.

THE PRIESTESS AND THE SKULL

Once there was a priestess, who kept watch over a skull on a rock in the sea. But one day, a wave swept the skull away. The priestess dived into the sea and swam after the skull for days until she reached an island. There she met the goddess Haua, who laughed when she heard what the priestess for looking for. Haua explained that the skull was Makemake, her husband.

The priestess was amazed by this news. She decided to stay with Haua and Makemake, and they fed her on the fish that they caught. Then, one day, Makemake suggested driving the sea birds to the island of Rapa Nui. Haua asked the priestess to come with them, and show the islanders how to worship the two gods.

Makemake and Haua drove the birds to their nests on the islets off the coast at Orongo, and the priestess taught the islanders how to honour the gods. She explained that before every meal, they must set aside a portion of food and offer it to Makemake and Haua.

THE BIRD-MAN

Rapa Nui's mythology is dominated by two things: the cult of the bird-man and the moai, the enormous head-and-torso stone statues, stone memorials to great chiefs.

Makemake, the creator god of Rapa Nui, was the patron of the bird-man cult. Each year, the clans gathered at the sacred village of Orongo, and waited for the arrival of the sea birds. The islanders believed the birds were driven to the island by Makemake. Each chief sponsored a swimmer to brave the waters in a race to collect the first bird's egg of the season. The chief to whom the egg was presented became the bird-man, the living representative of Makemake for one year.

After centuries in which the settlement on Rapa Nui thrived, the islanders eventually found themselves trapped. Clearing the forests to create land for agriculture, they had left themselves without wood to build ocean-going boats, such as outrigger canoes.

A CULTURE IN DECLINE

By the time Captain Cook (1728–1779) visited the island in 1774, the culture that had raised the great stone moai was in decline. Inter-clan warfare had toppled many of the moai. Famine, deforestation and warfare had reduced the population to a state of wretched poverty. The islanders were so demoralized that they traded away the holy images of their gods.

In 1862, Peruvian slave-traders raided Rapa Nui and stole away 1,000 islanders. Only 15 islanders survived to return to the island, but they brought smallpox with them. By 1872, there were only 110 islanders left, and 1,000 stone moai, staring out over a barren waste.

Today, the descendants of these first few survivors still value their island culture and honour their first ancestor Hotu Matu'a. They also continue to hope for the return of the great stone moai – the Friend Which Has Been Stolen – taken from Orongo, and now housed in the British Museum in England.

PACIFIC OCEAN

Aluluei figurehead guarding a canoe

MICRONESIA

IFALUK ISLAND

MELANESIA

POLYNESIA

PAPUA NEW GUINEA

TIKOPIA ISLAND

Bluetongue Lizard

AUSTRALIA

Great Murray cod

INDIAN OCEAN

NEW ZEALAND

Mapusia

TIKOPIA ISLAND

AUSTRALASIA & ⬩ OCEANIA

Australia is home to the oldest continuous civilization on earth, that of the Aboriginal peoples. The profound subtlety of Aboriginal mythology is only just beginning to be appreciated. The island groups of Melanesia, Micronesia and Polynesia in the Pacific Ocean are also rich in myth.

THE GODS' WORK

Tikopia is one of the Solomon islands in the southwest Pacific Ocean. It had a population of about 1,200 in 1928, when its traditional rites were still performed. Although Tikopia is in Melanesia, Tikopia culture is essentially Polynesian, and its ritual cycle, known as the Work of the Gods, has affinities with rites such as the inasi of Tonga.

Tikopia has always been vulnerable to ferocious tropical cyclones, which have usually been followed by famine, as the fertile ground is soaked by salt water and takes at least three years to recover. In December 2003, the island was devastated by Cyclone Zoë. Whole villages were swept away, but no lives were lost as the Tikopia have learned by experience how to cope with cyclones. They leave their homes and take refuge on higher ground.

APPEASED WITH GIFTS

The purpose of the Work of the Gods was to maintain contact with the atua, powerful spiritual beings whose favour was required to feed the Tikopia and guard their health. These gods and spirits were appeased with gifts of food and drink, and asked with elaborate formality to make the breadfruit or yam harvest plentiful.

The Work of the Gods was divided into two parts: the Work of the Trade-Wind and the Work of the Monsoon. One of the sacred dances of the monsoon season was the Taomatangi, the dance to quell the wind. The atua were believed to be present at this dance, sitting with their backs against sacred stones, the male atua cross-legged, the female atua with their legs straight in front of them. When the anthropologist Raymond Firth (1901–2002) took photographs of this dance, the Tikopia were surprised that the gods were not visible to the camera.

The major rites of the Work of the Gods included the re-dedication of the sacred canoes, the re-consecration of the temples, harvest and planting rites, a sacred dance festival, and the ritual manufacture of turmeric. Blood-red turmeric – used as ritual body paint and as a sacred dye – is said to be the perfume of Mapusia, the principal atua of Kafika, one of the four Tikopian clans; the yam (yams, above) is said to be his body.

The Work of the Gods was a logical system of trade with the spiritual beings. The Tikopia performed the rituals for the gods, and in return the gods granted the Tikopia the necessities of life. The complex cycle of ritual performances lasted for six weeks, twice a year. The Tikopia as a people kept the intricate sequence of these performances in their heads, and ensured that they were carried out correctly. To play one's own part in the ritual cycle brought status and pride.

A STRUCTURED SOCIETY

In the Work of the Gods, the Tikopia developed a system in which ritual performance and economic activity, such as food production, were inextricably combined. The Work of the Gods was literally what held Tikopian society together.

Through the 20th century CE, the Tikopia were gradually converted to Christianity. At first the new religion sat alongside the old, but gradually the rites dwindled away, and the Work of the Gods was abandoned in 1955, after an epidemic in which 200 people, including the Ariki Kafika and other chiefs, died. There were simply not enough believers left for the old system to work, and the remaining pagan chiefs converted to Christianity.

Each rite of the Work of the Gods required food to be offered to the atua. The bulk of this food was then consumed by the participants in the rite. The main sacrifice was of the time and energy required to perform the ritual, rather than of food. And even the time and energy were not spent without reward, for many of the actions required by the rites were economically valuable. The rituals involved such work as plaiting mats, making thatch (right) and repairing canoes.

Navigating the seas

The coral atolls of Micronesia are often described as paradise islands. These coral reefs in the Pacific Ocean support small populations in relative ease, and enable them to develop societies notable for peacefulness and creativity.

Inspiring gods

When the USA took over the Trust Territory of Pacific islands – including the Caroline, Marshall and Mariana islands – after World War II, at least one Caroline atoll, Ifaluk, had never had a resident missionary. Although the total population of Ifaluk was only 250, a visiting anthropologist collected from them a long book of very beautiful poetry. Everyone on Ifaluk, it seemed, was a poet, though they attributed their inspiration to one or other of their gods, being themselves only 'canoes of the gods'.

Ifaluk is a ring of coral around a lagoon, with only 0.3km² of land. It grows abundant coconut, breadfruit and other fruits and vegetables. As with other Pacific cultures, fishing in outrigger canoes has sustained the population with fish from the sea. The design of the Ifaluk canoes is ascribed to the god Aluluei, the god of navigation, and the canoes are always painted red, black and white. Aluluei has two faces – one looking forward, and one looking back – so that he can see both where a canoe is heading and any dangers that threaten it from the rear.

The beach is a favourite place for Ifaluk children to play. It is through play that they learn the essential Ifaluk values of co-operation and non-aggression.

To navigate the seas around Ifaluk, it is necessary to memorise the route by reference to the stars (Ifaluk father teaching his son to navigate, right).

A FAIR TRADE

One morning, Aluluei's daughter saw a large canoe in the sea. In it were three gods: Valur, the god of fish; Werieng, the god of birds; and Segur, the god of sea captains. She waded out to the canoe with a tiny coconut in her hand, no bigger than her fist.

'Come aboard,' they said. 'We are so grateful to you for giving us that coconut, we shall give you a chart of the sea. It marks all the islands, all the birds and all the fish.'

The girl took the chart to her father. Even though Aluluei was a great navigator, he did not know all the information that was on that chart. Aluluei showed the chart to the people, and taught them all the lore of the sea. And that is how the art of seamanship came to Ifaluk atoll.

Traditionally, both Ifaluk men and women tattoo their bodies; in the case of the men, the tattoos cover the whole upper body and flanks. This practice was said to have been instituted by the trickster god Wolfat. He came down from the sky to court a human woman, who fell in love with him because of his beautiful tattooing. Therefore, the men tattoo themselves using black soot, etched onto the skin with a needle made from the wing bone of a man-of-war bird.

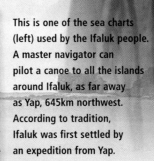

This is one of the sea charts (left) used by the Ifaluk people. A master navigator can pilot a canoe to all the islands around Ifaluk, as far away as Yap, 645km northwest. According to tradition, Ifaluk was first settled by an expedition from Yap.

THE STARS AND THE WINDS

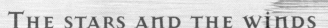

Ifaluk society is ordered by social rank which is fixed at birth, according to which of eight clans a child is born into. The only ways of rising in society are to become a master canoemaker, a navigator or the oracular mouthpiece of a god. Navigators learn a huge amount of lore about the stars, the winds, the currents and the life of the sea through an apprenticeship. Their ritual incantation states, 'I do not forget the guiding stars'. Most navigators also take on their canoes a wooden effigy of Aluluei, with the upper body of a man, but with stingray (fish) stingers instead of legs.

While Aluluei and other sea gods are perhaps closest to the daily concerns of the people of Ifaluk, many other gods appear in their poems. Most of the gods live in the sky of flowers with the great spirit Aluelap, his son Luguelang and his grandson, the trickster Wolfat. Aluelap made the sky, the ocean and the islands, and then the people to live in them.

The god who most frequently makes the journey from sky to earth is Tilitr, who descends to Ifaluk to inspire poetry, to warn of approaching evil, to rebuke bad behaviour and to help the people in times of sickness or famine.

THE DREAMING

The myths of the Aboriginal peoples tell of the doings of the great ancestors of humankind in the creation-time, the Dreaming. This time is not seen as the remote past, but as the true present. The Warlpiri people of central Australia call the Dreaming the Jukurrpa. The myths of the Jukurrpa are the sacred basis of all Warlpiri culture and law.

Government settlements were established for the Warlpiri when they were evicted from their lands. About 1,000 Warlpiri people still live in the largest of these, Yuendumu. However, increasing numbers of Warlpiri now live in outstations on their homelands, which have been reclaimed under the Land Rights Act for the Northern Territory.

The first Europeans entered the Warlpiri land in the middle of the 19th century. The 20th century saw both pastoral settlement of the land, and two gold rushes (settler panning for gold, left). A shortage of water in this desert environment caused friction between the Warlpiri and the miners and cattle farmers, and the Warlpiri were forcibly evicted from their lands.

KEEPING MYTHS ALIVE

Jukurrpa myths are intimately tied to the ancestral land on which the Warlpiri live. These tales, describing the wanderings of the ancestors from place to place, combine to create a map in story form of the Warlpiri land.

Every Warlpiri person inherits responsibilities for the nurture of the land from their father. Part of this responsibility is the duty to keep the myths of the Jukurrpa alive through song, storytelling, dance, ritual, and by paintings on the sand or on the human body. In recent years, Warlpiri painters have expressed the myths of the Jukurrpa through vibrant paintings on canvas.

A VISUAL CODE

Although their canvas paintings look like abstract patterns of colours, they are in fact re-tellings of the myths in a kind of visual code, in which each mark has a precise meaning.

Before the arrival of the Europeans in the 19th century CE, the Warlpiri lived entirely in the Jukurrpa, as their ancestors had done. Now they have to balance two opposing world views: their belief in the eternal present of the Jukurrpa, and the relentless forward movement of western society. The arrival of the Europeans is believed by the Aboriginal peoples to have brought about the end of the Dreaming as an everyday reality.

THE MAGIC FIRE

In the Jukurrpa, an old man and his two sons camped in Warlukurlangu, the place of fire. The old man, called Bluetongue Lizard, was a powerful sorcerer. He pretended to be blind, so that his two sons would bring back meat for him. But once they were gone, he would leave camp and catch his own food, which he did not share with them. He went hunting in Ngama, the cave of the rainbow snake, from which he gained his magical powers. But one day the two sons accidentally killed a kangaroo which used to talk to Bluetongue Lizard and tell him secrets. Not knowing it was sacred to the old sorcerer, they gave it to him to eat. Bluetongue Lizard was so angry that he summoned a magic fire and sent it after his sons. Everywhere they went, the fire pursued them, burning them. Every night it died down, but every morning it started up again, driving them all over the Fire country. At last, at the Ngarra* salt lake, they sank down, too exhausted to go further, and died.

The Warlpiri fire ceremonies are very dramatic. At the climax, the dancers are attacked and burned with flaming torches, just as the two young men in the Fire Dreaming myth are pursued by their father's magic fire. The ritualized aggression of the ceremony is used to settle old quarrels, and promote peace and friendship.

* Ngarra is one of the most sacred sites of the Warlpiri; only men may go there.

SACRED LAND

The Ngarrindjeri (pronounced Narrinyeri) are the Aboriginal people of the Lower Murray area in South Australia. Despite massive disruption to their traditional way of life since the foundation of the province of South Australia in 1836, the Ngarrindjeri retain a strong sense of their unique cultural identity and spiritual traditions.

The myth in which Ngurunderi pursues a giant Murray cod down the Murray river, creating the river in the process and stocking it with fish, is the foundation stone of Ngarrindjeri culture. The river itself was the artery of the living body of the land.

When the Ngarrindjeri women tried to protect the sacred island of Kumarangk from exploitation, they could not say why, for the myths and rituals surrounding it were 'secret women's business', not to be revealed to any man.

CULTURAL VALUES

Prior to the arrival of the Europeans, the Ngarrindjeri had the highest population density in Aboriginal Australia. Today, the 3,000 people of Ngarrindjeri descent do not live a tribal life, but retain many of the cultural values of their ancestors. Most are now Christian, but many have reached a balance between their Christian faith and their Ngarrindjeri beliefs. As with other Aboriginal peoples, the myths of the Ngarrindjeri centre around the actions of the ancestral creators in the Dreaming (see pages 134–135). Foremost among these is Ngurunderi, who founded Ngarrindjeri society, and shaped their land. The major ancestors of the Ngarrindjeri, including Ngurunderi, did not transform into animals or geographical features when they had finished their creative work; instead they went to live in a realm in the sky, Waiyuruwar, where they welcome the spirits of the dead.

One of the remarkable features of traditional Ngarrindjeri society is its high level of equality between the sexes. Nevertheless, both men and women had their own initiation rites and sacred knowledge. This divide between male and female knowledge became crucially important in the 1990s in a high-profile legal battle that set a political storm raging over the nature of Ngarrindjeri myths.

THE ADVENTURES OF NGURUNDERI

In the days of the Dreaming, Ngurunderi followed a great Murray cod down the length of the river in his canoe. Up to that time the Murray river was just a stream, but as the cod fled Ngurunderi, the movement of its tail created great bends in the river. On a sand shoal at the river mouth, where the sweet water meets the salt, Ngurunderi's brother-in-law Nepeli speared the cod and Ngurunderi cut it to pieces with his stone knife. As he cut each piece he threw it into the water, telling each piece to be a different kind of salt or freshwater fish. Then Ngurunderi lifted up his canoe* and put it in the sky.

One day, Ngurunderi's wives left him, and he set off in search of them. When he eventually caught up with his wives they tried to escape by wading out to Kangaroo island**, but Ngurunderi sent a tidal wave to drown them, and they turned into the rocks known as the Pages. After that Ngurunderi went across to Kangaroo island, dived into the sea, and rose, cleansed, into the sky. And still the spirits of the dead follow the tracks of Ngurunderi to Kangaroo island, dive into the sea, and rise up to join him in the sky.

*The Ngarrindjeri believe that the canoe can still be seen today as the Milky Way.
** Kangaroo island (main image)

At the centre of this row was mythological knowledge kept secret by Ngarrindjeri women about the sacred site of Kumarangk (Hindmarsh island) at the mouth of the Murray river.

The problem arose when developers wanted a bridge between Goolwa and Kumarangk. The state government committed to building the bridge, but the Ngarrindjeri objected. They asked the government to stop the bridge, and protect the island. The island and the waters around it, they said, had a sacred significance for them. The point where the sweet water of the river and the salt water of the sea meet represented their life force, and to allow the bridge to be built would be a disaster.

The bridge was built, and the sacred living body of the Ngarrindjeri land suffered a cruel blow, not just to its ecosystem, but to the web of spiritual power at the heart of its culture.

137

Osiris

EGYPT

Amun-Ra

Hapy

Aido-Hwedo

Benin

Atlantic Ocean

Southern
Africa

/Kaggen

Kalahari
Desert

AFRICA

Africa is a patchwork of tribes and cultures
where more than 1,000 languages are spoken.
The background to all African mythology
is the natural world of wild animals, forest,
desert and savannah (grasslands). In Africa,
apart from in ancient Egypt where hieroglyphic
writing was invented, the traditions are oral: the
myths were only written down over the last two
centuries. The traditional African way of keeping
cultural records was through art and storytelling.

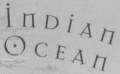

THE GOD OF MANY THINGS

The annual flooding of the River Nile, known as the inundation, was the most important event in ancient Egypt. Between June and September each year, the Nile swelled with water from the summer rains in the highlands of Ethiopia. The whole of Egypt's rich civilization depended on the inundation, and its deposit of new, fertile silt for planting crops along the riverbanks.

A POT-BELLIED GOD

The ancient Egyptians worshipped the inundation as the god Hapy. He was depicted as a pot-bellied man with sagging female breasts. Hapy was thought to live in a cavern at Aswân, where the flood first became noticeable. His myth explains that the flood poured from his cavern, 'making the meadows laugh'.

No temples were raised to Hapy, so he is often regarded as a minor god in the crowded Egyptian pantheon.

Hapy (left) lived in a cavern among the rocks at Aswân. When it was time for him to 'flood forth', the door of the cavern was opened by the ram-headed god Khnum, who shaped humankind on his potter's wheel.

RESTING IN THE OCEAN

According to one myth, the ouroboros, the cosmic serpent, lay coiled inside Hapy's cavern. It was the symbol of eternity and the endless renewal of time. The ancient Egyptians believed that this serpent was curled around the whole world. They thought that the waters of the flood were no less than the waters of the primal ocean, which covered the world at the beginning of time.

In releasing these waters, the serpent repeated, each year, the basic story of creation, in which the flood receded to reveal the land. Such repetitions, ensuring renewal, were central to Egyptian religion.

The serpent was the original form of the Egyptian creator god. He had rested in the primal ocean before time began, and would, according to the ancient Egyptians, rest in the ocean once more when time, and therefore the world, came to an end.

The rising height of the flood was measured using a nilometer (above). This structure was similar to a well, but with water levels marked on a central pole. Records were kept of the maximum height of the flood each year.

TWO GODS IN ONE

To the ancient Egyptians, Hapy could be either a minor god, representing the annual flooding of the River Nile, or the creator god, represented by the ouroboros, the cosmic serpent. Some pharaohs, such as Tutankhamun (see page 143) in the 18th Dynasty, had statues carved depicting them as Hapy, whose annual flood was one unchanging feature in the 3,000-year story of ancient Egyptian culture.

HAPY'S HYMN

Before the building of the Aswân dam in 1971, modern Egyptian Muslims believed that on the 17 June, the Night of the Drop, a miraculous tear drop fell into the Nile and caused it to rise. The rising of the Nile was announced in the streets by special Criers of the Nile, whose words of praise to Allah echoed the words of the ancient hymn to Hapy.

The ancient Egyptians were always threatened by famine. Since the Aswân dam was built, the annual Nile flood no longer occurs. The controlled irrigation of the land allows three crops to be grown where only one could be grown before.

Kingdom of the Sun

Ancient Egyptian texts tell of more than one million gods – so many, they could not accurately be counted. But all of them were simply aspects of the creator god, who called himself Atum, the all. The two most important of these gods were the sun god Ra, and Amun, the great god who listens.

The gods Amun and Ra

Where the interests of two gods coincided, they merged into a single god, such as Amun-Ra. But where two elements of a god contradicted each other, they could separate again to be worshipped under their two different names. Managing this highly complex but very flexible religion was the role of the priests who ran ancient Egypt's temples.

Amun-Ra was worshipped as the creator of all things, who brought himself into being by saying 'I am!' At Karnak, he was regarded as the king of the gods, and a temple was built in his name.

Akhenaten abandoned the ancient capital of Thebes, the cult centre of Amun-Ra, and built a new capital at Amarna. This was devoted to the Aten as the sole god. Although Amarna was only occupied for less than 30 years, it was a large city, with a population of up to 50,000.

RA'S SECRET NAME

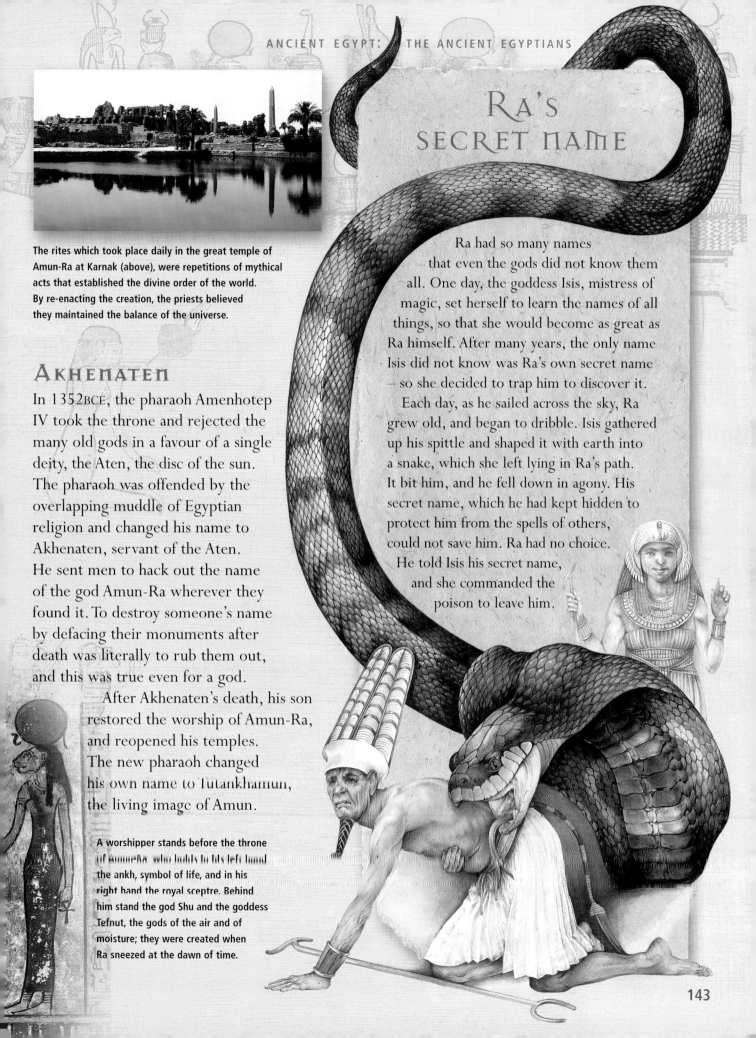

The rites which took place daily in the great temple of Amun-Ra at Karnak (above), were repetitions of mythical acts that established the divine order of the world. By re-enacting the creation, the priests believed they maintained the balance of the universe.

AKHENATEN

In 1352BCE, the pharaoh Amenhotep IV took the throne and rejected the many old gods in a favour of a single deity, the Aten, the disc of the sun. The pharaoh was offended by the overlapping muddle of Egyptian religion and changed his name to Akhenaten, servant of the Aten. He sent men to hack out the name of the god Amun-Ra wherever they found it. To destroy someone's name by defacing their monuments after death was literally to rub them out, and this was true even for a god.

After Akhenaten's death, his son restored the worship of Amun-Ra, and reopened his temples. The new pharaoh changed his own name to Tutankhamun, the living image of Amun.

A worshipper stands before the throne of Amun-Ra, who holds in his left hand the ankh, symbol of life, and in his right hand the royal sceptre. Behind him stand the god Shu and the goddess Tefnut, the gods of the air and of moisture; they were created when Ra sneezed at the dawn of time.

Ra had so many names that even the gods did not know them all. One day, the goddess Isis, mistress of magic, set herself to learn the names of all things, so that she would become as great as Ra himself. After many years, the only name Isis did not know was Ra's own secret name – so she decided to trap him to discover it.

Each day, as he sailed across the sky, Ra grew old, and began to dribble. Isis gathered up his spittle and shaped it with earth into a snake, which she left lying in Ra's path. It bit him, and he fell down in agony. His secret name, which he had kept hidden to protect him from the spells of others, could not save him. Ra had no choice. He told Isis his secret name, and she commanded the poison to leave him.

143

THE HALL OF JUDGEMENT

It is not true to say that the ancient Egyptians were obsessed with death. Rather, they were obsessed with life. All their rituals of death – mummification, entombment and ritual remembrance – were aimed at ensuring new life after death. They wanted to live forever in the Field of Reeds, where the blessed dead harvested in rich crops under the watchful eye of Osiris, the lord of the dead.

ETERNAL LIFE

The story of Osiris was the foundation myth that offered the ancient Egyptians the hope of a new life after death. At first, this was only for the pharaoh, who 'became' Osiris in the underworld, but eventually the promise of eternal life was open to all Egyptians.

To ensure this continued life in the Field of Reeds, the ancient Egyptians believed that care had to be taken of all the elements that went to make up a complete person – the physical body, the name, the shadow, and the ba and the ka which together are roughly the equivalent of what we call the soul. After death, they thought they would be led by jackal-headed Anubis into the Hall of the Two Truths.

The cult centre of the god Osiris (left) was at Abydos, where for over 2,000 years the mysteries of the god were celebrated. The myth of his murder was re-enacted, and at the end the djed-pillar, a stylized sheaf of corn which symbolized his rebirth, was erected. Tombs contained 'Osiris beds' – wooden frames in the form of Osiris, filled with earth and sown with seeds of barley, as a promise of new life to come.

The Field of Reeds was a perfected vision of Egypt. There, the dead were promised abundant harvests of barley and emmer wheat. Corn was sacred to Osiris, which is why the pharaoh himself cut the first sheaf of the annual harvest.

THE RULER OF THE DEAD

Osiris once ruled as a king on earth. He taught the Egyptians many skills, such as how to grow crops, and how to make and use tools. But his jealous brother Seth murdered him and cut his body into 14 pieces, which he scattered up and down Egypt.

Isis, the wife of Osiris, gathered up all the pieces save one, which was gobbled up by Sobek, the greedy crocodile god. Together with the ibis god Thoth and jackal-headed Anubis*, Isis put the body of Osiris back together, making the first mummy. But she could only restore Osiris to life long enough to conceive an heir, Horus. After that, Osiris had to return to the underworld to be the ruler of the dead.

* Anubis (right) helped to put Osiris back together.

THE WEIGHT OF THE HEART

The first Egyptian mummies were created by nature. When the bodies were buried in the hot sand, the body tissue dried out, rather than rotting away. This preserved the body and

created a 'natural' mummy. It may have been this discovery that gave the ancient Egyptians the idea of preserving human tissue.

The embalmers removed the lungs, stomach, intestines and liver prior to mummification. But they always left the heart in the body. They believed the heart of the deceased was weighed on scales against the feather of maat, the feather of truth, in the Hall of Two Truths.

If the heart, heavy with evil thoughts and acts, weighed more than the feather of maat, it would be gobbled up by the monster Ammut, the devourer of the dead. This terror avoided, the deceased was led into the presence of Osiris and the other gods for judgement. Only when the gods were satisfied could the spirit of the deceased enter the Field of Reeds.

Desert nomads

The San people, who are also known as the Kalahari Bushmen, are among the oldest inhabitants of southern Africa, with a culture that stretches back at least 30,000 years. Indeed, according to their mythology they were the first people who ever lived on earth. They speak a language punctuated with hard-to-pronounce clicks (which appear as '/' in this text) that are said to be traces of the earliest human tongue.

Once, the San were widespread across southern Africa, from the Cape to Kenya – the evidence for this is their famous rock paintings (antelopes, above) that were created wherever they went. But tragically most of their land was taken from them, and is now used by many international mining and agricultural corporations.

In 1999, the Xhomani San people won a major land claim from the South African government, giving them control of 65,000 hectares of the Kalahari desert. However, the government in Botswana is still trying to evict the San from their traditional hunting grounds in the Central Kalahari Game Reserve, to make way for tourism and diamond mining.

HUNTER-GATHERERS

The San are nomads, who live in clan groups of about 100 people, each speaking its own dialect. Today, they are to be found mainly in the hostile wilderness of the Kalahari desert – in Namibia, Botswana and South Africa – where they are able to survive using their incomparable skill as hunter-gatherers.

About two-thirds of the clan group's food is foraged by the women, who find edible roots, berries and delicacies such as the white pupae of termites, known as 'Bushman rice'. The men hunt animals, such as the large spiral-horned eland antelopes, using arrows tipped with poison.

The San's myth-drenched view of the world as a place in which the supernatural and the natural are inextricably entwined still has a haunting power. The motto '!Ke e:/xarra //ke' on the new coat of arms (left) of the Republic of South Africa is in the now-extinct /Xam language. It means 'people who are different join together'.

/KAGGEN'S ELAND

/Kaggen, the mantis, took a piece of his son-in-law Kwammang-a's shoe, and turned it into the first eland. He called the creature to him and rubbed the eland with honey to make it shine. Every time /Kaggen returned, the eland had grown, and when he saw it, /Kaggen sang for joy.

But his cunning grandson Ichneumon discovered the eland, and told his father. Kwammang-a hunted and killed the eland. When /Kaggen arrived, he wept to see his son-in-law cutting up the eland meat. In anger, he pierced the eland's gall-bladder with a stick, and darkness poured out, covering the world. /Kaggen then created the moon. It is under the light of the moon that men hunt; but the eland, once so tame, is now wild and difficult to catch.

THE LAST OF THE SAN

The San believed in a supreme being, who created all things, and to whom they prayed for success in hunting, for rain, or for relief from illness. One of the names of this creator god is /Kaggen. He was a trickster, who was envisaged as a man much like the San, but he could change himself into any form. /Kaggen's favourite forms were a mantis and an eland antelope.

The San believed /Kaggen created the world by dreaming it into being. San shamans entered this same creative dream-state to exercise their powers, such as rain-making. /Kaggen loved the elands, and it was said that only these antelope knew where he was – no man ever did. /Kaggen, the trickster, sometimes tried to divert the attention of hunters to give a shot eland time to recover from the effects of the poisoned arrow-head and make its escape.

The San were excellent storytellers. A vast collection of narratives of the Cape Colony /Xam San, one of the many San groups, was written down in the 1870s, from /Xam who had been imprisoned in Cape Town for such 'offences' as stealing a sheep to avoid starvation.

The /Xam San culture and language are now extinct; famine and persecution had made their traditional life unsustainable by the middle of the 19th century CE. But other San groups in the Kalahari desert, though still subject to harassment, continue to live their traditional life.

THE WILL OF MAWU-LISA

The ancient West African kingdom of Dahomey (now the republic of Benin) developed one of the richest mythologies in Africa, and also one of the most coherent; for the royal family made a deliberate effort at the beginning of the 18th century CE to centralize and organize Dahomean religion. Yet there are still so many gods and cults that no one has ever been able to systematically list them all.

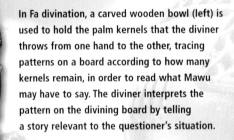

In Fa divination, a carved wooden bowl (left) is used to hold the palm kernels that the diviner throws from one hand to the other, tracing patterns on a board according to how many kernels remain, in order to read what Mawu may have to say. The diviner interprets the pattern on the divining board by telling a story relevant to the questioner's situation.

The Fon trace their history back to a legendary ancestor, Zogbo (Dahomey figure, right), who crossed the desert to live in Dahomey with his wives Heti and Heto. A Fon proverb says that if someone says he is greater than another, ask him, 'Are you Zogbo?'

TWO FACES

The chief people of Dahomey are the Fon. Their myths are similar to those of their near neighbours, such as the Yoruba of Nigeria and the Ewe of Togo. They share, for instance, a religious cult, called Fa by the Fon, in which various vodun, gods, are summoned to aid and advise the people. Traditional religion is at the centre of Fon life. Through Fa ceremonies, they can learn the will of Mawu, the creator. Mawu is one person with two faces: the first is a woman, Mawu, whose eyes are the moon; the second is a man, Lisa, whose eyes are the sun. So the creator is often called Mawu-Lisa. The word mawu means 'god' in Fon.

Mawu-Lisa gave birth to many gods, including Gu (left), the god of iron, and Legba, the trickster, who is the only one of Mawu's children who remembers the language of heaven. That is why both gods and men must go through Legba if they want to approach Mawu.

DEITIES

Aido-Hwedo, the rainbow serpent, also takes a twinned male-female form, which is common to many Fon deities. Aido-Hwedo is said to have come into the world with the first man and woman, Adanhu and Yewa, who were created by Mawu.

A second Aido-Hwedo lives in the sky, as the rainbow, and transports the thunderbolts of the gods to the earth. Aido-Hwedo means 'you are both in the earth and in the sky'.

CREATOR

When Mawu made the world, Aido-Hwedo carried her everywhere in his mouth. That is why the earth curves and winds, because it was shaped by the movement of the serpent. When Mawu had finished making the world, she saw that there was too much of everything; the earth needed something to rest on. So Aido-Hwedo was told to coil into a circle and support the earth. Mawu made the sea for Aido-Hwedo to rest in. Sometimes the earth chafes him, and when he shifts, he causes earthquakes. Aido-Hwedo eats iron bars that are forged for him by red monkeys that live beneath the sea. When the iron runs out, hunger will drive him to gnaw his own tail. Then the earth, with all its burdens, will tip into the sea.

The two Aido-Hwedo serpents are foremost among the Fon gods who travelled with slaves from Benin to the West Indies, to become the gods of Haitian voodoo. In Haiti, the male snake is called Dambala Wèdo, and his female consort is called Aylda Wèdo. They are the gods of wealth, luck and happiness.

✦ Other Mythical Figures

Europe

GREEK:

Eros
The god of love; born out of chaos at the dawn of time.

Hephaistos
The crippled god of fire and metalworking, husband of Aphrodite.

Herakles
A great hero, the son of Zeus by a mortal woman, Alkmene; famous for his 12 Labours. After death he became a god.

Hermes
The messenger of the gods; regarded also as a god of fertility and prosperity, he was the father of the god Pan.

Icarus
The son of the inventor Daidalos, Icarus plunged into the sea when he flew too close to the sun when the pair were escaping from Crete.

Midas
A Phrygian king who was granted the 'golden touch' by a grateful Dionysos.

Orpheus
A great musician, son of Apollo by the **Muse Calliope**; he failed to win his wife, Eurydice, back from the underworld.

Pan
The god of shepherds, flocks and the wild countryside.

Pandora
A woman, in the form of a goddess, made from clay by Hephaistos, to marry Epimetheus, brother of **Prometheus**. Her dowry was a jar which, when opened, let out all the diseases and ills of the world.

Perseus
A great hero, son of Zeus; he cut off the head of the **Gorgon Medusa**.

Prometheus
A Titan whose name means 'forethought'. He created the first human beings from clay, and stole fire from the gods for them. His brother was Epimetheus, 'afterthought'.

The Furies
The goddesses of vengeance and retribution.

The Gorgons
Three monstrous women whose gaze could turn a man to stone; the snake-haired Gorgon Medusa was slain by the hero **Perseus**.

The Muses
The nine goddesses of the creative arts; they included Calliope, the goddess of epic poetry.

The Sirens
Enchantresses of the sea, half-bird, half-woman, who lured sailors to their deaths with the beauty of their songs.

ROMAN:

Aequitas
The goddess of fair dealing.

Angerona
The goddess of secrecy.

Anna Perenna
The goddess of the year; originally the sister of Dido, who followed Aeneas to Italy.

Atagartis
A Syrian fertility goddess. Her myth was like that of Inanna/Ishtar; the name of her consort was Dushara.

Bel
The Syrian sky god, worshipped at Palmyra, Syria and in Rome, in a triad with Iarhibol, the sun god, and Aglibol, the moon god.

Bellona
The goddess of war, the wife of Mars.

Castor and **Pollux**
Twin gods of protection and salvation.

Consus
The god of the granary.

Diana
The goddess of wild nature and hunting, and protector of women, identified with the Greek goddess Artemis.

Fides
The goddess of good faith.

Fortuna
The goddess of fate and luck.

Janus
The god of beginnings (hence the first month of the year is January), and also of gates and doorways; the first god to be named in a list of gods in a prayer.

Juno
Originally the Etruscan goddess Uni, Juno was the wife of Jupiter; she was identified with the Greek goddesses Hera and Rhea.

Ops
The goddess of plenty.

Quirinus
A Sabine war god, worshipped in triad with Jupiter and Mars.

Sabazius
A Thracian god associated with Cybele, the Magna Mater, and identified with Bacchus.

Terminus
The god of boundaries.

CELTIC:

Brigit
Irish goddess of healing, divination and poetry, the daughter of the Dagda; now venerated as St Brigit.

Cernunnos
The Celtic lord of the animals.

Lugh
The Irish sun god.

Morrigán
The Irish triple war goddess; she sometimes transforms into a raven or crow.

Nantosuelta
A goddess of fertility, the wife of the Gaulish hammer god Sucellus; her name means 'winding river'.

VIKING:

Aegir
A god of the sea; married to Ran.

Honir
The silent god; one of the Aesir, sent as a hostage to the Vanir in the war between the two groups of gods.

Kvasir
The wisest of all beings, made from the spittle of all the gods of the Aesir and the Vanir to seal their truce; Kvasir was murdered by dwarfs and his blood was made into the mead of poetry.

Mimir
The god of wisdom and prophecy.

Skadi
Daughter of the giant Thiassi; she married the sea god Njord.

Surt
The fire giant who will burn up the world in the final battle of Ragnarok.

FINNO-UGRIC:

Illmarinen
The craftsman god, who forged the sky and magical Sampo.

Luonnotar
The daughter of nature, an air girl, mother of Väinämöinen.

SLAVONIC:

Byelobog and **Chernobog**
The western Slavic dual gods of good and evil.

Khors
The sun god.

Rod
The god of the family.

Volos
The cattle god.

ASIA

MESOPOTAMIAN:

Adapa
The legendary ruler of Eridu, the earliest Sumerian city, who refused the gift of immortality.

Baal
Canaanite sky god.

Lugalbanda
A shepherd-king of Uruk who was married to the goddess of wild cattle, Ninsun. Lugalbanda and Ninsun were the parents of the hero Gilgamesh.

Nanna
The Sumerian moon god; called Sin by the Babylonians.

Utu
The Sumerian sun god; called Shamash by the Babylonians.

INDIAN:

Agni
The god of fire.

Bara Deo
The Baiga god of bewar agriculture.

Buddha
Gautama (c.563–480BCE) was a great sage who achieved enlightenment and founded the Buddhist religion; he is said by Hindus to have been one of the ten avatars of the god Vishnu. The stories of previous lives of Buddha are told in the Jataka.

Durga
The terrifying form of a female warrior with 1,000 arms taken by the goddess **Parvati** to vanquish a demon of the same name.

Garuda
The king of the birds.

Indra
The god of the skies, thunder and lightning.

Inga
Singpho mud-girl who became the earth.

Kali
The goddess of death and birth.

Kama
The god of love.

Krishna
The eighth avatar of Vishnu.

Mahadevi
The great goddess; the goddesses Uma, **Parvati**, **Kali**, and **Durga** are all aspects of the great goddess.

Mu
Singpho cloud-boy who became the sky.

Parvati
The mountain goddess of the Himalayas; the wife of the god Shiva; also called Uma.

Yama
The god of death.

OTHER MYTHICAL FIGURES

ASIA

JAPANESE:

Aeoina-kamuy
The Ainu culture hero; also called Ainurakkur.

Benten
The goddess of music and the arts; one of the seven gods of luck.

Kotan-kor-kamuy
The Ainu creator.

Tsuki-yomi
The moon god, son of Izanagi and brother of Susano.

CHINESE:

Chang E
The moon goddess; wife of the archer **Yi**.

Xi He
Wife of the lord of heaven, Di Jun, and mother of the ten suns.

Xi Wang Mu
The Queen Mother of the west; the wife of the Jade Emperor.

Yi
The divine archer who shot down nine of the ten suns.

SIBERIAN:

Tangen
Co-creator of the world with Raven; Raven stole the sun from him.

THE AMERICAS

NORTH AMERICAN:

Awonawilona
'The ones who hold our roads', the most powerful of the Zuni Raw People.

Big Black Meteoric Star
The Pawnee master of the buffalo and controller of the night; Big Black Meteoric Star gave the Pawnee shamans their sacred medicine bundles.

Born for Water and **Monster Slayer**
The culture heroes of the Navajo (Diné), the sons of the sun and **Changing Woman**.

Changing Woman
Diné goddess of life and creation; grows old then young each year.

Eagentci
Old Woman, the earth mother in the mythology of the Iroquois tribes, such as the Seneca.

First Creator and **Lone Man**
The dual creators of the Mandan; First Creator turned into Coyote.

Four Beings of the North
The Four Beings provide food for the Pawnee.

Glooscap
Glooscap and his twin brother Malsum, the wolf, are the dual creators of the northeast coast.

Morning Star
The most powerful of the stars in Pawnee mythology.

Qayak
The Alaskan Inuit transformer, hero of a cycle of creation-time adventures.

Sky Holder and **Flint**
The children of Eagentci in Iroquois mythology; they are rivals in the creation of the world.

Wakan Tanka
The great mystery; the creator or life force in Lakota mythology.

Wakanda
The invisible life force that permeates all things in Omaha mythology.

Winabojo
The trickster and culture hero of the Algonquian nations; also known as Nanabozho.

MESOAMERICAN:

Chalchiuhtlicue
The Aztec goddess of rivers and standing water; the wife of **Tlaloc**.

Ehecatl
The wind god; an aspect of Quetzalcoatl.

Huitzilopochtli
The supreme deity of the Aztecs, associated with sun and fire.

Itzamna
The Maya lord of the heavens, husband of Ix Chel, the goddess of childbirth and healing.

Ometeotl
Aztec god of duality, the ultimate source of all creation.

Tlaloc
Aztec god of rain and lightning.

Toci
Old Woman, the Aztec earth goddess.

Yum Cimih
The Maya lord of death.

SOUTH AMERICAN:

Haburi
The culture hero of the Warao of Venezuela.

Kóoch
Sky, the creator of the Tehuelche of Argentina.

Kúwai
Culture hero of the Cubeo of Brazil.

Mamacocha
The Inca sea and water goddess, the wife of Viracocha

Nothing But Bones
The creator of the Baniwa of Brazil.

Pachamama
The Inca earth goddess.

Pillan
The thunder god of the Araucanians of Chile.

Pulówi
The underground mother of the game animals of the Guajiro of Colombia.

Tokwah
The trickster, culture hero and lord of the dead of the Mataco of the Gran Chaco.

Wanadi
The creator and culture hero of the Yekuana of Venezuela.

Watawinéwa
Supreme deity of the Yamana of Tierra del Fuego.

Yoálox brothers
The culture heroes of the Yamana of Tierra del Fuego.

Oceania and Australia

POLYNESIAN/MELANESIAN MICRONESIAN:

Autran
The goddess of the earth and mother of humankind on Ifaluk atoll in the Caroline Islands.

Bego Tanutanu
Bego, the maker, the culture hero of the Mono-Alu of the Solomon islands.

Geb
A giant whose body became the earth and whose head became the sun in the mythology of the Marind-anim of Papua New Guinea.

Metikiki
The culture hero of Tikopia.

Papa
Mother earth in Maori mythology.

Rangi
Father sky in Maori mythology.

AUSTRALIAN:

Biame
The all-father of southeastern Australia.

Djanggawul
The Dreaming ancestors of the Yolngu people of Arnhem Land.

Lumaluma
The Dreaming ancestor and culture hero of the Gunwinggu people of Arnhem Land.

Mamu-boijunda
The great spider who, with Jarapiri, the rainbow serpent, created the world of the Warlpiri of central Australia.

Matamai
The son of Ngurunderi in the mythology of the Ngarrindjeri of south Australia; he was the first being to die.

Mimi spirits
Miniature Arnhem spirit people.

Ungambikula
The Dreaming ancestors of the Aranda of central Australia.

Africa

EGYPTIAN:

Bastet
The cat goddess.

Bes
A popular god of good fortune.

Geb
The earth goddess.

Hathor
An important goddess who was regarded as the mother of the pharaoh.

SUB-SAHARAN AFRICAN:

Aberewa
The earth spirit of the Akan-Asante, Ghana.

Ajok
The supreme being of the Lotuko, Sudan.

Ala
Mother earth goddess of the Ibo of eastern Nigeria

Dxui
Another name for /Kaggen, the creator of the San of southern Africa.

Gamab
The supreme being of the Berg Damara, Namibia.

Leza
The supreme being of the Ila-speaking peoples of Zambia.

Nkulunkulu
The Zulu supreme being, South Africa.

Obatala
Supreme being and sky god of the Yoruba, Nigeria.

Oduduwa
The earth goddess of the Yoruba, Nigeria.

Uhlakanyana
The miniature trickster of the Zulus, South Africa.

Yurugu
The jackal trickster of the Dogon, Mali.

Glossary

agriculture The practice of growing crops for food.

alluvial valleys Formed by silt deposited on flat land by a fast-flowing river.

ambrosia The nectar of the gods, which gives eternal youth.

amulet A small object worn as a protective charm.

annexed Taken without permission.

archaeological evidence Knowledge gained by excavating ancient sites.

artery A vessel that carries blood from the heart around the body; in some myths, a river is seen as the artery that carries the lifeblood of a landscape.

assassinated Killed in a planned killing.

baptised Received into the Christian church by the rite of baptism, an immersion in water.

barbarian A word used by a civilized people, such as the ancient Romans, for a people they consider uncivilized.

bureaucracy A system of government based on rules and regulations, or the officials of such a government.

carpenter A craftsman skilled in woodwork.

cavern A large cave hollowed out by water.

census An official count of the population.

chess A game of skill, played with pieces on a board, in which the aim of the two players is to capture each other's king.

city-state A state centred on one important city that rules the outlying land, towns and villages.

civilization The art of living in cities. Used to mean a sophisticated society, or an entire culture.

condemned Sentenced to punishment or pronounced to be guilty.

conquer To overcome another country in war, possibly to invade and rule it.

continental plates 200 million years ago the continents of the world were part of a single landmass, called Pangaea. Since this broke up, the rigid layers of land (plates) that make up the continents have moved.

cosmic Relating to the whole **universe**.

cosmos The world or **universe**.

creation-time The era in which mythical beings shaped and transformed the world.

cult The system of worship of a particular god or religion.

cyclone A violent tropical storm; also called a hurricane.

dam A barrier built across a river to restrain the water.

deity (pl. **deities**) A god or goddess; some deities may have no gender, or be both male and female.

delta The flat area at the mouth of a great river where the mainstream divides into a number of lesser streams.

desert Dry land with little vegetation and low rainfall.

divination The art of foretelling the future by magical powers or practices.

dormant Quiet and inactive.

dynasty A sequence of hereditary rulers.

earthquake A shaking of the earth.

elixir A drink giving eternal life or youth.

empire A number of separate territories or countries under the rule of a single person or state.

epic A long poem telling the story of a legendary hero; an heroic journey or undertaking suitable to each story.

equinox The dates in spring and autumn when day and night are of equal length.

eternity Endless time; forever.

etiquette The customs or rules of correct behaviour in a particular situation.

evangelical mission A group of people sent to a foreign country to convert the people to Christianity.

evergreen tree A tree that does not lose its leaves in winter.

excavated Carefully dug up by an archaeologist.

excreted Discharged from the body as waste material.

famine A shortage of food, often caused by a failure of the crops due to lack of rain.

fertility The growth of plants and crops, or the reproduction of animals or humans.

fleet A group of ships.

flood plains The flat area beside a river, onto which the river floods and deposits silt.

foothills The lower hills at the foot of a mountain range, or the lower slopes.

fords Places where it is shallow enough to cross a river without building a bridge.

frescoes Wall paintings.

garrotting Execution by strangling.

genealogies Lists of ancestors stretching back in time.

genocide A policy of killing the members of a particular ethnic group.

glacier A mass of ice.

gold A precious metal.

Grand Duchy A state ruled by a prince known as a grand duke.

guardian spirits Spirits that protect an individual, household or society; often associated with ancestors.

hieroglyphs Pictures or symbols used in some forms of writing, as in ancient Egypt.

highlands A mountainous area.

humanity The human race as a whole.

humankind The human race.

hunter-gatherer A society that lives by hunting animals and gathering wild food.

igloo A house built from ice by the Inuit.

illiterate Unable to read or write.

illusion Something that is believed to be real but is not.

immortal Living forever.

incense Any sweet-smelling substance that is burned during religious rituals or ceremonies in honour of a god.

indigenous Original to a particular country.

inter-clan A clan is a group of people who are related to each other; some societies divide into a number of clans, and any relations between the clans, whether friendly or hostile, are inter-clan.

lawmaking The establishment or rules by which a society agrees to live.

leap day An extra day added to the calendar every four years to allow for the difference between a solar year (365.2422 days) and the calendar year (365 days).

lunar Relating to the moon.

maggots The larvae of insects such as flies.

manifestation The appearance in visible form of a god or spirit.

meditation Spiritual contemplation.

Meiji Restoration The reign of Emperor Mutsuhito (1867–1912) during which Japan opened up to the western world.

mid-Atlantic ridge An area of earthquakes and volcanic activity beneath the Atlantic Ocean stretching between Iceland and the Antarctic Circle.

municipality An area of local administration in Mexico.

murdered Deliberately killed.

mystery Something which cannot be understood. A mystery religion is one in which the rites are kept secret.

navel On a human body, the point at the centre of the abdomen where the umbilical cord was attached; more generally, the very centre of something.

navigation The art of sailing accurately from one place to another.

nomadic A nomadic people moves from place to place in a yearly cycle, rather than settling in one spot.

oracle A prophecy revealed by the priest or priestess of a god, or the **shrine** at which prophecies are made.

otherworld The world of the gods or spirits; sometimes, the world of the dead.

paganism The following of a pre-Christian religion; more recently, having no religion at all.

pantheon All the major gods of a religion.

parliament A political assembly authorized to make laws on behalf of a people.

pastoral settlement A place where people live and farm animals.

peasants People who work the land but do not own it.

pilgrims People who make a journey for religious reasons, usually to visit a **shrine**.

populous With many inhabitants.

primal The first of its kind; or something that existed at the beginning of time.

psychopathic Mentally unbalanced with a tendency to violence.

quartz A shiny mineral found in rocks, often as colourless rock crystal.

quest A search for something important.

raids Hostile attacks.

realm A country, kingdom or domain.

regeneration Bringing back to life.

republic A country ruled by representatives of its people, rather than a king or emperor.

resurrection A return to life from death.

rituals Formal acts and words enacted or spoken for religious purposes.

rum A strong alcoholic spirit distilled from sugar cane.

runes The letters of the Viking alphabet, used for divination as well as writing.

sacrifice The ritual killing of an animal or person in honour of a god; or the actual or symbolic surrender of wealth to the gods.

saffron A yellow dye from the crocus flower.

sage A wise man.

seafaring Sailing across the sea for trade or exploration.

settlers People who move to a new area.

shaman A man or woman who can communicate with the world of the spirits and has healing powers.

shrine A place of worship or sacred site.

smallpox A dangerous disease.

sorceress A female magician.

summit The very top of a hill or mountain.

superhuman Like human but more powerful.

supernatural Something that cannot be explained by the laws of nature; relating to the spirit world.

supreme Most powerful.

taboo Forbidden.

tattooer Someone who decorates the bodies of others with designs pricked on the skin and stained with indelible colours.

temple A building in which a **deity** is worshipped.

territory Land.

tribe A distinct group of people with a common culture, language and descent.

tropical Belonging to the hot countries situated between the Tropics of Cancer and Capricorn.

tuberculosis A serious infection usually affecting the lungs.

Uluru A great sandstone monolith in central Australia; formerly known as Ayers Rock.

underworld The world of the dead, often believed to be situated below the world of the living; sometimes called hell.

universe The whole world including the stars and planets.

usurp To take over the rule of a country from its rightful ruler, by cunning or force.

volcano A mountain formed by erupted magma from beneath the earth's crust.

voodoo Religious beliefs of African origin.

warfare Hostile relations between two or more peoples; waging war.

Index

ACKNOWLEDGEMENTS

The publisher would like to thank the following for permission to reproduce their material. Every care has been taken to trace copyright holders. However, if there have been unintentional omissions or failure to trace copyright holders, we apologize and will, if informed, endeavour to make corrections in any future edition.

Key: *b* = bottom, *c* = centre, *l* = left, *r* = right, *t* = top, *bkgd* = background

Pages: 2–3 Getty Images, London (Getty); 4–5*bkgd* Corbis; 4*tr* Bryan and Cherry Alexander/Arctic Photos (Arctic Photos); 4*b* Royal Geographical Society/Alamy; 5*br* National Geographic Society Image Collection (NGS); 6–7 NGS; 12*tl* Corbis; 12*c* Bridgeman Art Library, London (BAL); 12–13 Corbis; 13 Mary Evans picture Library (MEPL); 14*tl* Werner Forman Archive (WFA); 14*r* Corbis; 15*l* Art Archive; 15*cr* Corbis; 16–17*bkgd* AKG, London (AKG); 16*tl* Getty News; 16*b* Corbis; 17*l* BAL; 17*tr* BAL; 18*tr* Art Archive; 18*c* Corbis; 18–19 Getty; 19 Corbis; 20*tr* Corbis; 20–21 Corbis; 21*tl* Corbis; 21*cr* Art Archive; 22*l* Art Archive; 22–23 Deutsche Press Alliance, Germany; 23*t* Art Archive; 23*b* WFA; 24*tl* BAL; 24*cl* Art Archive; 24*r* BAL; 25*tl* Corbis; 25*cr* Art Archive; 28–29*bkgd* AKG; 28*bl* BAL; 28*tr* BAL; 29*tr* Art Archive; 29*cl* BM; 29*b* AKG; 30–31*bkgd* AKG; 30*tl* Art Archive; 30*c* AKG; 31*tr* AKG; 31*c* AKG; 31*bl* AKG; 32*tr* Art Archive; 32*cl* Art Archive; 32–33 AKG; 33*tr* AKG; 34–35*bkgd* AKG; 34*tl* Scala; 34*br* AKG; 35*tr* AKG; 35*br* Art Archive; 36–37 Getty; 36*l* AKG; 38–39*bkgd* Corbis; 38 Corbis; 39*tl* Art Archive; 39*br* BM; 40–41*bkgd* AKG; 40*cr* AKG; 40*bl* AKG; 41*tl* Corbis; 41*br* Scala; 42*tl* BAL; 42*c* AKG; 43*tl* Scala; 43*bl* AKG; 43*br* Alamy; 44–45 Getty; 44*tl* AKG; 45*tl* BAL; 45*br* AKG; 46*tl* Art Archive; 46*br* Art Archive; 47*tr* AKG; 48–49*bkgd* Corbis; 48*l* Art Archive; 48*tr* Art Archive; 49*tl* BAL; 49*bl* Scala; 50–51*bkgd* Art Archive; 50*tl* Art Archive; 50*br* Corbis; 51*t* Art Archive; 51*l* Art Archive; 51*r* Art Archive; 52–53*bkgd* Art Archive; 52*bl* Art Archive; 52–53*t* WFA; 53*bl* Art Archive; 53*br* Art Archive; 54 Getty; 56*bkgd* Corbis; 56*bl* BAL; 56*tr* Corbis; 57 Art Archive; 58*tl* BAL; 58*br* Art Archive; 59*l* BAL; 59*tr* WFA; 60*tr* Swedish National Museum, Sweden; 60*b* Art Archive; 61*tc* BAL; 61*r* Corbis; 62 Corbis; 63 Vladimir Fomin, St Petersburg; 64–65 NGS; 64*tl* Art Archive; 64*c* Art Archive; 68–69*bkgd* Getty; 68*cl* MEPL; 68*r* BAL; 69*tl* Art Archive; 69*cr* Corbis; 70*tr* Corbis; 71*tr* Corbis; 71*bl* Getty; 71*br* Corbis; 72–73*bkgd* Scala; 72*tl* Art Archive; 73*cr* Corbis; 74*tr* Art Archive; 74*cl* Art Archive; 74–75 British Library (BL); 75*tr* AKG; 76*tr* Getty; 76*cr* BL; 76*b* Corbis; 77 Corbis; 78*tl* BL; 78–79*b* BL; 79*tr* Art Archive; 80*tl* Link, London/Dinodia of India; 80–81 Corbis; 81*tl* Corbis; 82–83 Alamy; 82*tl* Corbis; 82*b* Corbis; 83*c* Corbis; 83*b* Corbis; 84–85 Corbis; 84*tr* Corbis; 84*cl* Corbis; 84*br* Corbis; 86–87 Colin Nicholas, Center for Orang Asli Concerns, Malaysia; 86*tl* Colin Nicholas, Center for Orang Asli Concerns, Malaysia; 87*tl* Colin Nicholas, Center for Orang Asli Concerns, Malaysia; 87*b* Colin Nicholas, Center for Orang Asli Concerns, Malaysia; 88*tl* Corbis; 88*cr* Corbis; 88*bl* Corbis; 90*tr* Corbis; 90*cl* BM; 90*br* Corbis; 91*b* Corbis; 92–93*bkgd* Corbis; 92*tl* Corbis; 92*br* Corbis; 93*tc* Corbis; 93*b* Corbis; 94–95 Lonely Planet Images; 94*tr* Corbis; 94*cl* BM; 94–95*b* Corbis; 95 Corbis; 96–97*bkgd* Corbis; 96*tl* BAL; 96*bl* Corbis; 97 Asian Field reproduced with the very kind permission of the artist Antony Gormley and the White Cube Gallery, London/Press Association; 98*tl* BAL; 98*cl* BAL; 98*br* Corbis; 99*tl* Art Archive; 99*cr* Lonely Planet Images; 99*bl* Getty; 100–101 Getty; 100*tr* Arctic Photos; 100*cl* Arctic Photos; 100*bl* Arctic Photos; 101*tl* Corbis; 101*cl* Arctic Photos; 101*b* Getty; 104–105 Arctic Photos; 104*cl* Arctic Photos; 105*tl* Arctic Photos; 105*cl* Arctic Photos; 105*cr* WFA; 106*cl* Seattle Museum of Art/Corbis; 106*r* Getty; 107*tr* Seattle Museum of Art/Corbis; 107*bl* WFA; 108–109 Corbis; 108*tl* Library of Congress, Washington DC; 108*bl* Corbis; 108–109*b* Corbis; 109*tl* Corbis; 109*br* Corbis; 110–111*bkgd* Corbis; 110*tr* Corbis; 110*c* Corbis; 111*cl* Corbis; 111*br* Corbis; 112*tl* Corbis; 112*cr* Corbis; 112*bl* Corbis; 113*tl* Corbis; 113*tr* Ardea; 113*b* Corbis; 114–115 Art Archive; 114*tl* Art Archive; 114*tr* Art Archive; 114*b* BM; 115 WFA; 116–117 Corbis; 116*tr* Justin Kerr/MAYAVASE, New York; 116*cl* Corbis; 116*b* Art Archive; 117*b* Art Archive; 118–119 Getty; 118*tr* Corbis; 118*bl* Corbis; 119*tr* Getty; 119*c* Alamy; 119*bl* Corbis; 120–121*bkgd* Art Archive; 120*tl* Art Archive; 120*cl* Art Archive; 120*b* Art Archive; 121*t* WFA; 121*br* Art Archive; 122–123*bkgd* Getty; 122*b* Still Pictures; 123 Still Pictures; 124–125*bkgd* Corbis; 124 Corbis; 125*t* Corbis; 126*tr* NGS; 126*b* NGS; 130–131 Still Pictures; 130*cl* Associated Press; 130*br* Panos Pictures; 131*t* BM; 131*b* Corbis; 132–133 Corbis; 132*cl* Corbis 132*br* Corbis; 133*c* BM; 133*tr* Corbis; 134 Corbis; 134*c* Corbis; 136–137 Corbis; 136*l* WFA; 136*tr* Alamy; 137*b* Alamy; 137*cr* Alamy; 140–141*bkgd* NGS; 140*l* AKG; 140–141 Corbis; 141*t* Corbis; 142–143*bkgd* Art Archive; 142 Art Archive; 142*br* Art Archive; 143*tl* Art Archive; 144–145*bkgd* Art Archive; 144*l* AKG; 144*br* Art Archive; 145*t* Art Archive; 146*cl* Corbis; 146–147 Corbis; 148–149 WFA; 148*cl* BAL; 148*cr* Corbis; 149*tl* BAL; 149*b* BAL; 150–151 Alamy; 152–153 Alamy

Covers: *front cover* British Museum (Quimbaya funeral mask, Columbia, CE600–1100); *back cover* British Museum (Aboriginal bark painting, Australia); *back cover flap* British Museum (Indian painting, Bengal, c.CE1800)